SILENT CONVERSATIONS

SILENT CONVERSATIONS

Reading the Bible in Good Company

WILLIAM APEL

Judson Press
Valley Forge

Silent Conversations: Reading the Bible in Good Company

© 2000 by Judson Press, Valley Forge, PA 19482-0851

Library of Congress Cataloging-in-Publication Data

Apel, William D.
  Silent conversations : reading the Bible in good company / William Apel.
    p. cm.
  Includes bibliographical references.
  ISBN 0-8170-1320-2 (pbk. : alk. paper)
  1. Bible Reading. 2. Christian biography. 3. Bible Criticism, interpretation,
etc. I. Title.
BS617.A64 2000
220.6′1—dc21   99-059130

Printed in the U.S.A.

06 05 04 03 02 01 00   10 9 8 7 6 5 4 3 2 1

To generations of students
who have graced my life with good company
and to my family, Jane, Emily, Paul,
who have filled my life
with joyful conversation and love beyond words

❧ CONTENTS

PREFACE

Great is the LORD, and greatly to be praised.

Thou hast awakened us to delight in Thy praise;
for Thou hast made us for Thyself, and our heart
is restless, until it finds its rest in Thee.

St. Augustine, *Confessions*

So often we are left to our own devices when trying to read the Bible for its meaning and spiritual guidance. Like St. Augustine, the great bishop of the ancient church in North Africa, we frequently read the Scriptures alone and in silence. Such practice of silent reading without moving the lips was novel in Augustine's Roman world, but for us it is commonplace. Yet like Augustine, alone in the solitude of the early morning or late evening hours, we too meditate upon the Bible searching for what God has to say to us in the myriad of circumstances that form our lives.

Of course, numerous biblical commentaries and study guides can help us break open God's Word. Bible study groups abound and often are instructive and edifying. But in the quiet times, alone with our Bibles, we sometimes long for more immediate help. At these moments, alone with God, we are nurtured by the Holy Spirit. But I have also discovered others to be present in my silent solitude. These companions for silent conversations down through the centuries have been called the communion of saints. Perhaps Augustine himself experienced a comparable reality—what the writer of Hebrews in the New Testament refers to as being "surrounded by so great a cloud of witnesses" (Hebrews 12:1).[1]

Throughout the years, perhaps as a result of teaching courses on Christianity at college and in the church, the communion of saints has become real to me. In my times of silent Bible reading, I have turned again and again to those I deem saints and sages of our faith for insight and inspiration. They have become lasting friends as we silently converse about the meaning of this or that biblical passage. Speaking from their time and place, these men and women of faith have granted me a perspective on God's Word that I would otherwise not have. Remarkable insights can be and have been derived from encountering the Bible in this way. Reading the Bible in the good company of the communion of saints is what this book is all about.

In the following pages, the reader is invited to open the Bible in the good company of saints and sages of our faith, both ancient and modern. Imagine! At your side is gathered a host of silent partners for Bible study representing many of the great figures of Christianity—men and women such as Augustine, Julian of Norwich, Martin Luther, John Wesley, Dietrich Bonhoeffer, C. S. Lewis, Howard Thurman, Madeleine L'Engle, Thomas Merton, Martin Luther King Jr., Mother Teresa, and Desmond Tutu. We are indeed "surrounded by so great a cloud of witnesses."

In Augustine's time and within monastic groups today, Christians have regularly practiced *lectio divina*, a kind of spiritual reading.[2] Kathleen Norris, a contemporary poet and Benedictine oblate, has described this sort of meditative reading as "an attempt to read more with the heart than the head." Similarly, in *The Good Book*, Peter Gomes of Harvard has reminded us never to forget to read the Bible with both heart and mind. But this requires of us a different approach to reading. First, it takes patience—something hard for many of us to master. We must learn to wait upon the Lord. In the second place, we must learn how to brood over a passage of Scripture. This approach involves something like what Robert Raines has termed "creative brooding." Many times college students have complained to me that they are "not getting any-thing" out of their reading assignment. I listen and then ask them how many times they have read the assigned passage. The frequent response, "once," gains another response from me, "only once?" The Bible, especially the Bible, is a demanding book. We serve ourselves best by returning many times to the same passage, looking each time for more wisdom. The Bible is like a treasure buried in the field. We have to dig for its deeper truth. And when we find it, we rejoice! This is what the saints and sages, men and women of profound faith, have done in their *lectio divina* for century upon century.

Many sources besides this book can provide lengthy and necessary academic and intellectual support for reading the Bible. However, this work is primarily concerned about something else. Its intent is to encourage a slow, meditative reading for personal inspiration. The chapters are relatively brief and self-contained. Each can provide for hours of reflection and creative musing. With heart and head, we will declare with the psalmist, "Great is the LORD," and greatly to be praised." My hope in this writing is that your silent conversations will lead you further into the depths of God and the service of others.

The chapters in this book are arranged so that the reader's meditations may be as direct as possible. Each chapter begins with a Bible passage and a quote from the writings of one of our saints or sages. The Bible passage and the words from the saint or the sage should be read slowly and thoughtfully. A prayer is encouraged before reading the remainder of the chapter. Next, the chapter ponders and probes the Bible passage itself. After this, we examine how and why this particular passage of Scripture is so important to the experience of our silent companion. In the process, we will consider the implications of God's Word, and that of the faithful cloud of witnesses, for our own journeys. The arrangement of the chapters is thematic rather than historical. I have taken my cue for organization from the apostle Paul and have ordered these chapters under the headings of the theological virtues of faith, hope, and love (1 Corinthians 13). In doing so, I have attempted to span the Bible from Genesis to Revelation. Our companions for silent conversation will alternate between modern and ancient as the chapters unfold. It is not possible in so small a book to be comprehensive in the Bible passages I have chosen, or in the selection of saints and sages. Nevertheless, I have chosen biblical passages and lives of saints and sages that I believe have a special word for our day. My linking of particular passages from the Bible with specific men and women of faith is not coincidental, for these very biblical passages are the ones through which God has spoken to the communion of saints before us. These witnesses have had their lives changed and redefined by their Bible reading—I am convinced it can happen to us as well—each in his or her own time and place according to the wonderful grace of God.

ACKNOWLEDGMENTS

WE ARE THE ILLUMINATION OF THE BRIGHTEST, and even the faintest, stars that chart the constellation of our lives. This is especially true in the writing of a book. I cannot begin to identify all the stars that have shaped, and continue to shape, my heart and mind. So many students, for example, have contributed to this work that it would be unfair for me to name some to the exclusion of others. But there is a sense in which every student I have ever taught has also taught me—and for this I can only say thanks.

I cannot imagine this present work without thinking of William Millar and Stephen Snyder, my two colleagues in religious studies at Linfield College. They have expanded my field of knowledge and have added to my intellectual and spiritual pursuits in ways that I may never fully understand. Their imprint is indelible. Also, I want to express gratitude to my colleague in anthropology, Joel Marrant, whose spiritual awareness has caused me more than once to rewrite a few of my chapters. These three are invaluable friends.

Other words of appreciation must go to Linfield College, its president Vivian Bull, and deans Marvin Henberg and Barbara Seidman, for their constant support of my academic and church endeavors. The gifted editors at Judson Press have added their talents to this work as well. I want also to thank Anna McCormick, who typed my manuscripts over and over—demonstrating some of the qualities of a true saint. It goes without saying that the book itself is fully my doing, and its shortcomings are my own. As brother John Wesley would say, we are all moving on to perfection. My journey, someday to be perfected by God's love, has many, many miles to go. Thanks to all who share in this particular pilgrimage, especially my family and my big brother Terry, to whom this work is especially dedicated.

WILLIAM APEL
Linfield College and the Trappist Abbey
Advent 1999

PART ONE

Responding in Faith

CHAPTER ONE

The Sign of Jonah

Now the word of the Lord came to Jonah son of Amittai, saying, "Go at once to Nineveh, that great city, and cry out against it; for their wickedness has come up before me." But Jonah set out to flee to Tarshish from the presence of the Lord.

JONAH 1:1–3

The sign Jesus promised to the generation that did not understand Him was the "sign of Jonas" the prophet—that is, the sign of His own resurrection. The life of every monk, of every priest, of every Christian is signed with the sign of Jonas, because we all live by the power of Christ's resurrection. But I feel that my own life is especially sealed with this great sign . . . like Jonas himself I find myself traveling toward my destiny in the belly of a paradox.

THOMAS MERTON, *The Sign of Jonas*

THE SIGN OF JONAH (or Jonas) is a sign of contradiction. The story is somewhat familiar to many of us. Jonah is called forth by God to preach judgment against the foreign city of Nineveh for its wickedness. The reluctant prophet responds by heading for Tarshish, which is in the opposite direction from Nineveh. Along the way, he is caught in a storm at sea, swallowed up by a great fish, and after three days and nights in the belly of the sea creature, he is unceremoniously regurgitated onto dry land. A second time the word of the Lord comes to Jonah to go to Nineveh. This time he does. Much to Jonah's surprise, the people of Nineveh repent, God changes his mind, Nineveh is saved. This angered Jonah: he demanded judgment, but God preferred compassion and mercy.

Why Jonah?

Why begin our silent reading in the middle of the Bible? Why start with Jonah? Why a sign of contradiction? We begin with Jonah because this ancient prophet is so much like most of us—filled with contradictions and often finding God to be likewise. Jonah, like us, wants things to go his way. What results for him is a conflicted life and a troubled relationship with God.

Almost everything within the book of Jonah is debated by biblical scholars. Precise dating and authorship, as well as meaning, seem uncertain in this wonderfully told story of ancient Israel. But within the brief forty-eight verses of this most unique of Israel's prophetic writings, we find a true soul mate. Who hasn't been in Jonah's predicament? Who hasn't felt confused and conflicted? Jonah's dilemma is our dilemma: how to cope with life when things don't go our way and God doesn't seem at all helpful.

Jonah could not understand God, so he resisted God at every turn in the story. He did not want to go to Nineveh; someone else could preach to the violent Ninevites. Jonah's solution to God's calling was to run in the opposite direction. During a storm at sea, he is thrown overboard by sailors he managed to alienate, and then he is swallowed by a great fish. After three days and three nights, poor Jonah is spewed out on dry land. Kicking and screaming, the ever-so-reluctant prophet finally concedes to go to Nineveh. We can sympathize with Jonah by this point in the story. He has been tossed and shaken to his core—and literally hung out to dry by a persistent and overpowering God. Jonah never really had a chance; he was going to Nineveh one way or another. God's will was not about to be thwarted. And if this were the entire story, we might be left with a God who is something of a cosmic bully.

However, in a most remarkable passage of Scripture, God changes his mind and has compassion on the Ninevites. The Almighty refuses to bring down the destruction he had threatened. God repented (*naham* in Hebrew). Many English translations of Jonah 3:10 obscure this detail, perhaps for theological reasons. But the old King James version had this one right: "And God saw their [the Ninevites'] works, that they turned from their evil way; and God repented of the evil, that he had said that he would do unto them; and he did it not."

God repents for the sake of compassion and mercy. God is responsive to the people's repentance. This divine change of direction, from destruction to mercy, places compassion above judgment. It turns out that the primary nature of God is to love, and so, compassion overflows. For Jonah, this is the proverbial last straw. Since God will not orbit around Jonah's little universe, Jonah is angered. God will not bend to Jonah's will and fall into line with the way in which the stubborn prophet wants things to go. In Jonah's mind, this recalcitrant Deity will not even follow established religious procedures. The Ninevites deserve punishment for their sins of wickedness and violence. This is required for the sake of righteousness by the sovereign One of Israel. Jonah is certain from his religious upbringing that he has this point right! He may have been wrong in his initial refusal to go to Nineveh, but the religious message of righteousness was clear. Like Sodom and Gomorrah, Nineveh had earned its judgment for past wrongs. Let the ax fall!

God's mercy was a sign of contradiction *for* Jonah. What confusion! First, he is in the belly of the fish, lost to life, only to be spewed back from death to life. Then, in Nineveh, God's compassion and mercy seem to have gone haywire. A whole people saved. Bewilderment? A puzzlement for Jonah. This God is too confusing. Redemption is occurring before the prophet's own eyes, but his sense of religious propriety blinds him. He cannot see because he cannot see beyond himself. Even at the end of the story, Jonah remains intractable. He is more concerned about the loss of his little shade bush than he is about the fate of thousands of souls in Nineveh. The day of salvation has come for the Ninevites, and Jonah is more worried about a sunburn.

As far as Jonah was concerned, God could not be trusted. The prophet had been pushed about, dumped in the sea, swallowed by the sea creature, but none of this matched the utter humiliation Jonah felt when in his esteemed estimation God did not back his preaching in Nineveh. This was too much of a contradiction for Jonah. If God could act like this, what else might God do?

Centuries later the answer came back. Another prophet spoke of God's amazing forgiveness and mercy in a manner that confused his entire generation. Whereas Jonah had protested God's compassion, this prophet embraced it and even embodied it. When asked for a sign of clarification, this prophet who was more than a prophet replied that the only sign to be given his generation was "the sign of Jonah" (Matthew 16:4). Jesus knew we all live with the sign of Jonah.

As with our silent companion Thomas Merton, to whom we now turn, we each live in "the belly of a paradox." Contradictions still exist in our lives. God may elude us at times, and we are often swallowed up by our own selfish concerns. And life and death are jumbled together in confusing patterns. But we are not fated to remain Jonah forever. For as Thomas Merton, and countless others, have discovered down through the ages, the sign of Jonah is also the sign of Christ's resurrection—a hidden sign for new life and a renewed faith.

Thomas Merton: Out of Silence

Living with the sign of Jonah is something that Thomas Merton, the Trappist monk, knew all too well. In the annals of Christian history, no individual has explored the meaning of the sign of Jonah more deeply and more personally. For this best known of all Catholic writers in the twentieth century, the paradoxical sign of Jonah became the central biblical truth that was to shape his witness to contemplation in a world of action. As Merton himself stated, "The life of every monk, of every priest, of every Christian is signed with the sign of Jonas, because we all live by the power of Christ's resurrection." However, for Merton, as with Jonah, the path to God's shining truth was often filled with darkness and contradiction. It frequently seemed hidden from view by our own obstinacy. But what was so remarkable about Merton, and instructive for us, was his awareness that even in the darkness and contradictions God was present.

Born in Prades, France, in 1915, Thomas Merton spent the first half of his fifty-three years in the noisy secular world of Europe and America, and the second half in the silent religious world of the cloistered Trappist monks at the Abbey of Our Lady of Gethsemani near Louisville, Kentucky. His life reads something like that of a modern-day Jonah. In the early years of his life, Merton seemed as determined as Jonah to run in the opposite direction from God. By the age of fifteen, he had lost both parents to disease and death. His maternal American grandfather dutifully supported his educational efforts at Cambridge University in England.

Unfortunately, Merton's start in higher education at Cambridge in 1933 was a disaster. It seemed his unquenchable thirst for intellectual stimulation was matched only by his desire for all kinds of experiences—most notably hedonistic ones. When his grandfather learned of Merton's low grades, carousing, and the pregnancy of a young woman, he ordered Merton to America. Enrolled subsequently at Columbia University in New York City, Merton found the intellectual and cultural climate there more to his liking. In this setting, he became a successful student and a promising writer and journalist. But any semblance of real purpose or direction was missing. An avowed atheist, young Tom Merton was on a Jonah-like flight from God.

Thomas Merton was a prototypical individual of the modern age: urbane, skeptical, cultured, and above all rootless. He prided himself on being a member of a "lost generation." He took comfort in throwing up his hands in despair. Like most skeptics, he refused to hope, for such realities seemed only to lead to greater disappointments. Better to be safe in a life devoid of meaning than to risk the foolishness of faith and the falseness of hope.

Then, something happened to change Merton forever. Following a brief association with campus communists, he and a small group of friends became interested in Catholicism and Catholic writers. At first this was only another intellectual curiosity, but in August of 1938 Merton began attending Mass at "the little brick church of Corpus Christi, hidden behind Teachers College on 121st street." Later he would write in his best-selling autobiography, *The Seven Storey Mountain:* "What a revelation it was, to discover so many ordinary people in a place together, more conscious of God than of one another: not there to show off their hats or their clothes, but to pray, or at least to fulfill a religious obligation, not a human one."[1]

Was this the beginning of Merton's turn toward Nineveh? It is quite difficult to identify that almost imperceptible moment when life turns Godward. In any case, Merton was overwhelmed by the thought that people could be "more conscious of God than of one another." More than a decade later, after becoming what Merton called "a grown-up monk," he realized that a contemplative consciousness of God included other people. However, in 1938 it was enough for Merton to break through to acknowledge God's existence. The rest would come later.

Merton was to learn that God is not in a hurry. As did Jonah, the young Merton became increasingly aware of God's persistence. This hound of heaven moved Merton to be baptized into the faith at Corpus Christi in November 1938. What came next shocked even his closest friends. Merton was now determined to enter a religious order, and he eventually joined the austere, silent Trappists of Gethsemani Abbey in December 1941. Merton had definitely turned toward Nineveh, or had he?

Life is so very difficult to chart when we are in the midst of it. The course is often far from clear; the mapping itself may be a problem. And so it was for Merton. In the first decade of his life as a Trappist, Merton believed himself to be truly on the path that God had ordained for him. Through the monastic disciplines of prayer (both communal and private), manual labor, and devotional study, he discovered a spiritual framework for what previously had been an unruly and disordered life. In his early writings (including *The Seven Storey Mountain*), encouraged by his abbot at Gethsemani, Merton's pious tones even suggest contempt for the world he left behind—a world of war and violence, of greed and shallowness. It is as if he rejected the world outright. In *Seeds of Contemplation,* written during these early years of monastic triumph,

Merton contemplated the potentiality of his own saintliness. Indeed, the seeds of contemplation that God had planted in his life seemed about to blossom. These were halcyon days for Merton, who relished his newfound life in God.

> Every moment and every event of every man's life on earth plants something in his soul. For just as the wind carries thousands of invisible and visible winged seeds, so the stream of time brings with it germs of spiritual vitality that come to rest imperceptibly in the minds and wills of men. Most of these unnumbered seeds perish and are lost, because men are not prepared to receive them: for such seeds as these cannot spring up anywhere except in the good soil of liberty and desire.[2]

Such beautiful and inspired prose is indicative of the spiritual seeds that had grown and blossomed within the monk Thomas Merton. By voluntarily committing himself to God in a rigorous monastic life, Merton experienced a freedom and a joy he had never known before. And through his popular devotional writings, thousands upon thousands of readers also benefited. Many of his works created a modern *lectio divina* bringing many people, especially young people, closer to God.

But what of Nineveh? Had Merton really turned toward God's destination for him, or was Nineveh in the other direction—in the world he had left behind? The geography of our spiritual lives is a tricky thing: just when we think we've got it, God seems to change the compass face once again.

In *The Sign of Jonas,* first printed in 1952, Merton shows evidence that Nineveh, wherever it was, still haunted his consciousness. He mused, "like Jonas himself I find myself traveling toward my destiny in the belly of a paradox."[3] Where would God finally spew forth Merton? What was his destination?

Would Merton be dumped back into the world outside the monastery walls? After all, this was the true Nineveh that the young Merton sought to flee. Merton's vocation was clearly that of a monk, but his gifts were that of a writer for the world. The writer in him kept returning him to a past and a place (the world) that he as a monk had essentially abandoned. How to resolve this contradiction? As early as the epilogue to *The Seven Storey Mountain,* Merton had lamented about "this writer who had followed me into the cloister."

> He is still on my track. He rides my shoulders, sometimes, like the old man of the sea. I cannot lose him. He still wears the name of Thomas Merton. Is it the name of an enemy?
> He is supposed to be dead.[4]

Merton, now Father Louis, had struggled with this writer within him. Was he still a divided self? How was it all going to come together? This is the same kind of spiritual question we ask of ourselves.

Ironically, and God seems to love irony, it was the writer in Thomas Merton that gave voice to his emerging prophetic concern for the larger world. In *The Sign of Jonas*, Merton began to grasp the singular meaning of his life as monk and writer. The one cannot be divorced from the other, nor is the monastery completely separate from the world—the inside and the outside of our lives are part of the same creation. Oh, how Merton struggled with these issues. "It is not much fun," he wrote in his journal, "to live the spiritual life with the equipment of an artist."[5]

Indeed, it is never much fun at the point of spiritual transformation. Whether it is the ancient Jonah or the modern monk Thomas Merton, the passage is never easy. Through his contemplative life, Merton slowly and painfully began to rediscover the world in all its glory and all its sufferings—first through reading the Bible itself, and then through increasing contact with many in the outside world.

Merton and the Bible

In a sense, Merton came to the Bible late in life. This may provide some of us with a certain amount of consolation. Many people avoid the Bible because of bad experiences with zealous preachers who insist upon dogmatic readings of Scripture. Others have shied away from the Bible because they cannot see how this ancient book has anything to say to the present situation. Or some, like Merton, have gotten a late start on the Bible. In Merton's case, prior to the Second Vatican Council in the mid-1960s, the average Catholic Christian did little personal Bible reading. This was true of monks as well. Not much in Merton's experience would have lent itself to a personal and direct encounter with Scripture.

In *The Sign of Jonas*, Merton acknowledged his lack of Bible literacy through his early years of monastic training. "How little Scripture I used to read in the novitiate," he lamented. But that was soon to change. As a result of his own silent conversations with Christian writers in the ancient church, especially the desert fathers of early monasticism, Merton became aware of how central the Bible is for life and faith. He then began to read the Bible in earnest. Always, he looked for pearls of wisdom and truth in his meditative Bible readings—what might be called its deeper meaning. Merton discovered his own key for unlocking Scripture. It was the Bible's capacity for spiritual nourishment, which he believed carried the reader beyond mere facts and surface meanings. Again, in *The Sign of Jonas,* Merton noted:

> Merely to set down some of the communicable meanings that can be found in a passage of Scripture is not to exhaust the true meaning or value of that passage. Every word that comes from the mouth of God is nourishment that feeds the soul with eternal life.[6]

In his notes for a later book, *Opening the Bible,* Merton recorded ideas from Protestant theologian Karl Barth, which insisted that one cannot speak of God merely by speaking of humanity in a loud voice.[7] Merton knew from his own experience that it was God's Spirit that spoke to him through the Bible. It was not merely the rumblings of human beings. The Bible contained God's revelation. This is not to say that Merton rejected the work of modern biblical scholarship. Quite the contrary was true. However, he constantly looked beyond all human efforts to explain the Bible for the voice that might be God's.

Merton's attentive reading of the Bible awakened in him an ever broadening and deepening spiritual life. He experienced firsthand what happens again and again when the Bible breaks open for its readers. The world itself begins to look different. A new outlook is gained. According to Merton:

> By the reading of Scripture I am so renewed that all nature seems renewed around me and within me. The sky seems to be a pure, a cooler blue, the trees a deeper green, light is sharper on the outlines of the forest and the hills and the whole world is changed with the glory of God and I feel fire and music in the earth under my feet.[8]

These words from *The Sign of Jonas* are reminiscent of those of the ancient psalmist. Indeed, the psalms of the Israelites had special meaning for Merton, for he chanted them daily in community prayer. They contributed directly to his emerging biblical perspective. Also, he began reading carefully throughout Scripture, never settling for this part of the Bible over that part. He believed what he claimed with all his heart, "Every word that comes from the mouth of God is nourishment that feeds the soul with eternal life." The Bible had taken root in Merton. He could "feel fire and music in the earth."

The Road from Nineveh to Calvary

For Thomas Merton, the portion of the Bible that had special meaning was, of course, the book of Jonah. In it he found his own story. Its economy of words may have appealed to the poetic and contemplative

Merton. But the story itself was what attracted Merton. Merton was Jonah, the one who fled from God only to find himself unable to escape God's providential grasp. Out of his own experience, Merton could declare, "I know well the burnt faces of the Prophets and the Evangelists."[9] By reading Jonah, Merton became convinced that living with God was not as simple an act as it had once appeared. In turning to the monastery, Merton thought he had resolved issues between himself and God. Like many of us, Merton had attempted to resolve matters from his side of things, only to discover that God had a different agenda. In the monastery, Merton awoke to the fact that he continued to travel "in the belly of a paradox." The journey was not over. He had not reached Nineveh at all. Nineveh was once again in the opposite direction. Merton's monastic destination was only God's new point of departure. Ironically, the Ninevites God sent Merton to preach to were back in the world. Called to the monastery, Merton was now called back to the world.

In 1953 Merton was to hear God's calling for a second time. He was in Louisville to see about printing a postulant's guide for Gethsemani, when he had a Jonah-like encounter with God—only this time there was no flight. This epiphany turned Merton back toward the world—perhaps his true Nineveh. Later, in *Conjectures of a Guilty Bystander,* he wrote of this experience:

> In Louisville, at the corner of Fourth and Walnut, in the center of the shopping district, I was suddenly overwhelmed with the realization that I loved all those people, that they were mine and I theirs, that we could not be alien to one another even though we were total strangers.[10]

Here were the Ninevites—the foreigners, the strangers. But for Merton, they were no longer strangers. They all were to be loved. They were all loved by God. Merton had learned the greatest lesson of his life: no barriers existed between himself and others, all were united in God's love. This was the good news of God for Thomas Merton. If only people could fully understand the compassion and mercy of God. If only Jonah could have comprehended the limitless scope of God's love, then he might have accepted the Ninevites' transformation as his own possibility. It is never too late. Merton knew now that he was not only Jonah but also the Ninevites. With God there are ultimately no walls of division, no boundaries to compassion and mercy.

For the first time, Merton truly marveled at God's love for human beings without exception. "There is no way," he wrote, "of telling people that they are all walking around shining like the sun." Merton could no longer neglect the world—and although he kept his vocation as a monk, his renewed commitment to people resulted in a compassionate embrace of God's world beyond the monastery walls. "To think," wrote Merton, "that for sixteen or seventeen years I have been taking seriously this pure illusion [a separate holiness] that is implicit in so much of our monastic thinking."[11]

With this new orientation, indeed a second conversion, Merton became an active voice for peace, justice, and racial reconciliation during the cold war era of the 1950s and 1960s—all the while maintaining a transformed monastic life at Gethsemani. He reached out to men and women of good faith both within and outside of Christianity. He joined with Buddhist monks and secular writers, with all who were willing to work for peace, and justice, and reconciliation.

In this whirlwind of writing, however, Merton did not become a religious blur without definition. He knew that within his own spiritual center; grounded in the Word of God, encouraged by his monastic vocation, and companioned by Christ, he could now be his true self. As a twice blessed but still flawed human being, he lived boldly with Jonah's sign of contradiction—doubt mixed with faith, sin mixed with grace, death mixed with life. He was at peace, for he lived as one not without hope. The sign of Jonah had become for him the sign of Christ's resurrection. And he knew out of this affirmation that no person is beyond the reach of God's love.

The book of Jonah was Thomas Merton's bridge between his monastery home and his greater home with all humanity. When Merton died during a conference of Catholic and Buddhist monks and nuns in Bangkok, he had already found his way to this greater home. He had crossed the bridge from Jonah in the Old Testament to Jesus in the New Testament to the world at large. At the close of his life, he knew that the only sign that any generation can expect is the sign of Jonah, and with this promise and hope for new life he was content. Signed by Jonah, saved by Christ, sent to serve.

CHAPTER TWO

Parables and Prodigals

Then Jesus said, "There was a man who had two sons. The younger of them said to his father, 'Father, give me the share of the property that will belong to me.' So he divided his property between them. A few days later the younger son gathered all he had and traveled to a distant country, and there he squandered his property in dissolute living."

LUKE 15:11–13

Not with our feet or by traversing great distances do we journey away from you or find our way back. That younger son of yours in the gospel did not hire horses or carriages, nor did he board ships . . . when he journeyed to that far country where he could squander at will the wealth you, his gentle father, had given him at his departure. Gentle you were then, but gentler still with him when he returned in his need. No, to be estranged in a spirit of lust, and lost in its darkness, that is what it means to be far away from your face.

ST. AUGUSTINE, *Confessions*

THE PARABLE OF THE PRODIGAL SON begins as a story of alienation. We can identify with this parable of Jesus because we too, like the wandering son in Luke's account, have been to that "distant country" removed from those we love, from God, from our true selves. This plight of the prodigal son has captured the hearts and imagination of countless individuals down through the centuries, but none more so than Augustine of Hippo, the great Christian leader and theologian of the ancient church in North Africa. Indeed, his close identification with the character of Jesus' prodigal son makes him an excellent partner for our silent conversation as we meditate upon Luke 15:11–32, one of the world's best-known stories.

The Parable

According to Jesus, a father has two sons. The younger son asks for and receives his inheritance, which the father has divided between his two sons. The younger son quickly gathers his new wealth and leaves for a distant land where he squanders his fortune in reckless living. His extravagant behavior and excessive action gain him the title of "prodigal" in Christian tradition, although the term is not itself used in the Gospel account.

The younger son, tradition's prodigal, lost everything. During a period of famine, he must tend pigs for a local farmer in order to stay alive. This action violates his religion's laws of purity and pollution for he had come in contact with swine—ritually unclean animals. Furthermore, he breaks his family's code of honor by bringing shame upon his father's name through riotous living. The prodigal son is headed toward a downward spiral into oblivion. For all intents and purposes he is dead.

Then the story turns in an unexpected direction. We are told that the younger son "came to himself" (Luke 15:17). After returning to his senses, he decides to seek acceptance back into his father's household as a hired servant. He knew he did not deserve to return as a son.

Next comes the parable's greatest surprise. While the prodigal son is still far off, his father spots him and runs out to embrace him declaring, "let us eat and celebrate, for this son of mine was dead and is alive again; he was lost and is found!" (Luke 15:23–24). Jesus knew that his listeners would find this part of the story incomprehensible. In first-century Palestine, fathers did not show such emotion and initiative toward their children. It would have been fully out of character for an authoritarian patriarch to act in such a manner. The proper thing would have been for the son to come crawling back to the father.

Jesus had turned expectations upside down. This unusual father called for celebration when there should have been sackcloth and ashes. The elder brother had the conventional wisdom on this point. When he learned from a servant about his brother's warm welcome back into the family, he was filled with indignation. Where were the logical consequences to be suffered by the prodigal for his waywardness? Where was the guilt and punishment? A celebration, this was absolutely wrong!

The elder brother stewed in his self-righteousness. He had been faithful and loyal to the family. This should count for something, for a whole lot! But whatever valid points the elder brother might have had soon became distorted. He could see no further than his own hurt feelings of not being appreciated. In fact, the elder son was so angered that in a conversation with his father he could not even grant recognition of his brother as a brother but rather referred to him as "this son of yours" (Luke 15:30).

The father's compassion, however, remained constant. He loved them both, whether he was dealing with his wayward son or his stay-at-home son. According to New Testament scholar Dan Via, "The father not only goes out to the prodigal son; he also goes out to the elder brother."[1] This parent extended grace upon grace. His unconditional love flowed in all directions, whether it was merited or not.

God's Rule

By the close of the parable, there is no doubt that Jesus has introduced us to a different world, a whole new order, another set of values, an alternative way of viewing life. In this world, people can ruin their lives and still find forgiveness and acceptance. Things are turned around: the call for compassion is more important than the need to be right; mercy exceeds judgment. Conventional wisdom goes out the door: fathers are shown to love their children even when the children do not honor their parents. Hope is not lost even when individuals are consumed by self-centeredness or self-righteousness.

The new reality embodied in Jesus' parables is the kingdom of God. Jesus taught this kingdom, God's rule, had drawn very close. It is in our midst! In Jesus' teachings, parables (in Hebrew, *mashal,* and in Greek, *parabole*) are indicators of God's presence among us. Jesus wants his listeners to see and experience what he does—God's sovereign reign breaking in on earth.

Through his parables, Jesus longs for us to see what is just beyond our sight, to touch what is just beyond our reach. This kingdom of compassion and justice, forgiveness and peace, was more real to Jesus than his beloved Galilean hills or the rude presence of Roman soldiers. It pervades all of life for Jesus but remains hidden from view because of our spiritual blindness and selfish preoccupations.

For Jesus, however, the kingdom was and is fully present in this world—here and now. God is transforming life, and we are called to be a significant part of that change. New Testament scholar Robert Funk writes in *Honest to Jesus,* "For him [Jesus] the furniture of the world had already been rearranged."[2] The parables of Jesus attest to this truth. In fact, parables like the story of prodigal son are designed to get our attention, to awaken us to the stirrings of God in our daily lives.

Jesus intended through his parables to jolt us into awareness—to make us conscious of God's presence in a world being transformed by divine action. Parables use the language of everyday life, speaking of common human activities like meals, weddings, business transactions, and farming; but they are signaling to us something uncommon. The parables trumpet a new day that begins with Jesus, but its continuation involves our participation. Another New Testament scholar, John Dominic Crossan, provides a helpful summary about parables and the kingdom of God in the conclusion to *The Dark Interval,* a challenging book on parables. He writes:

> I have interpreted the stories of Jesus as parables intended to shatter the structural security of the hearer's world and therein and thereby render possible the kingdom of God, the act of appropriation in which God touches the human heart and consciousness is brought to final genuflection.[3]

A parable like that of the prodigal son ought to shatter our familiar and often unexamined ways of understanding life. For when we begin to view the world through the filter of Jesus' parables, our hearts are indeed touched by God. To hear the parable is to hear the voice of the parabler himself. Jesus opens our eyes.

More Than One Prodigal?

We have noted the element of surprise in Jesus' use of this parable. After all, who in Jesus' first-century Palestinian audience could have anticipated the father's overly compassionate response to the prodigal son? Now I want to add a further surprise to our *lectio divina* of this parable: I believe there is more than one prodigal in Jesus' story—especially from a spiritual point of view.

Rightfully we have identified the younger son as the obvious prodigal in Jesus' parable. Our dialog partner, Augustine, will do the same, as has most of church history. Without question, the wayward son in the parable is in every sense a prodigal. However, consider for a moment the not so obvious possibility that in their own ways the elder brother, and even the compassionate father, may be prodigals.

The definition for prodigal, as we've used it in this parable, is one who is reckless in actions and extravagant in behavior. The younger son is all that—and more. By drawing an extreme picture of this son's destructive activity, Jesus made sure that we not miss the point: the younger son *is* a prodigal in his careless and loose living. He has shown total disregard for his family's honor and for his own well-being. But may there be other extreme behaviors in the parable? Other prodigals?

The elder brother is reckless and extravagant in his overwrought response to his brother. The younger son may have squandered his wealth in a distant country, but the elder brother's attitude toward him is equally reckless. In an extravagant manner, he is willing to sever his relationship with his own flesh-and-blood brother. This has much more to do with his own wounded sense of pride than with anything the younger brother might have done.

The elder brother's sense of rightness was magnified into self-righteousness as he lamented, rather than celebrated, the return of his lost brother. The self-pity of the elder brother was extravagant beyond words. Dom Helder Camara has asked a poignant question about this part of Jesus' parable: the younger brother is saved from his vices, but who will save the older brother from his virtues?[4] We too are quite capable of becoming prodigal in our smugness. Heaven and earth may have to yield dominion when we are convinced that we are in the right. There is no person more dangerous, and more the fool, than the individual who will not listen to others because of his or her own sense of righteousness. The ultimate tragedy of Jesus' parable is that the elder brother remained alienated from the younger brother at the story's end. There is no resolution or reconciliation, and we are left to wonder (or to act?) in regard to this part of the narrative. Perhaps Jesus is trying to tell us something: the unresolved parts of his stories are our legacy. To whom do we need to be reconciled?

Finally, there is the father in the story. I don't know of others who consider him a prodigal, but perhaps we should. Most often, we have identified this forgiving father with God, and this would not be far from the truth, especially in terms of his unconditional love. The quote from Augustine's *Confessions* at the beginning of this chapter does exactly that. However, we must be careful not to overstate the case. In Luke's Gospel, verses 18 and 21 of chapter 15 reveal that the father in the story cannot be equated totally with God. Here, references are made to the younger son's appeals for mercy both to heaven (God) and to his father. They are viewed as separate entities.

But to suggest that the father is a prodigal—isn't that going a bit too far? Maybe not, if we consider that, according to the wisdom of Jesus' day, the unconditional love of this parent involved reckless and extravagant behavior. The father was willing to ignore his society's standards of parental propriety for the sake of compassion and mercy. He was willing to jeopardize his cultural position as family patriarch in order to run out to embrace his lost son. Love could not be constrained by social convention or even cultural norms.

On many levels, this act of compassion was a reckless form of behavior—potentially irresponsible to the structures of family life and their authority. His relentless love threatened to undermine the very way in which parents and children were expected to relate. But that is how Jesus' parables worked—always affirming the possibilities of new life, regardless of their threat to the standing order of things. Always pushing the envelope.

Jesus' parable made it clear that God's commitment, like the father's in the story, was to an ethic and spirituality of compassion. All other religious virtues must fit into this new pattern of love. Justice, peace, judgment, reconciliation—each of these dimensions of God's emerging kingdom stood in the service of this type of compassion.

In the end, the parable of the prodigal son, like God's sovereign reign, does not permit us to remain disengaged. This is the challenging truth of Jesus' teachings that individuals like Augustine came to understand. We must ask: In light of this parable, what does it mean to be reckless and extravagant in faith, in love, in service of God? Are we to squander our lives in self-destructive behavior like the younger son? Certainly not. Are we to squander our lives in self-righteousness like the elder brother? Certainly not. Or are we to give away our lives in love like the forgiving father? Yes, this is the way. But the question is always ours to answer. What kind of prodigal shall we be? Prodigal for whom—for what?

Confessions

The individual whom the church calls St. Augustine never considered himself a saint. He saw himself much more as a prodigal. We know this from his *Confessions,* a spiritual autobiography, penned late in the fourth century during his forty-third year. He wrote as the bishop of Hippo in North Africa (modern-day Tunisia). In this most famous of all Christian autobiographies, we quickly discover that Augustine viewed himself far more as a sinner than a saint.

In fact, Augustine's story reads like an expanded version of the biblical tale of the prodigal son. He judged his youthful years to be squandered in the pursuit of sensual pleasures and empty philosophies. And running throughout the *Confessions* are allusions to the biblical prodigal son. For example, Augustine speaks of his early years as a "journey" to the "far country" with its darkness and separation from God. Writer

Robert Ellsberg says as Augustine looked back he saw "nothing but a desert of sin: pride, sensuality, and concupiscence—an anxious grasping after empty pleasure."[5]

Like the prodigal son of the Bible, Augustine came from a good family. An African by birth, he was raised in Thagaste, North Africa, by a devout Christian mother, Monica, and a caring pagan father, Patricius. Although he was not Roman, the brilliant Augustine received a classical education and, much to his father's delight, was prepared to advance in the Roman world as a teacher of rhetoric. According to historian Maria Boulding, Augustine's future looked bright. She said of Augustine:

> He looked out at a prosperous Mediterranean country, at well-maintained roads gleaming white in the sun, at olive groves, orchards and vineyards, at municipal buildings and public baths. And everywhere was the stamp of Rome.[6]

Augustine did find success as a teacher in the Roman Empire, moving first to Rome and then to Milan by the time he was thirty. Had he lived, Augustine's father would have been proud of his son's upward mobility. However, internally Augustine was in darkness. He found no real meaning in life. He could not accept the simple, and often superstitious, Christian faith of his mother. And even though he casually followed the teachings of Manicheanism, a religious philosophy of good and evil, he could find no lasting peace.

However, the one philosophy Augustine did find to his liking, especially after his move to Italy, was Neo-Platonism. The Neo-Platonists, like Plotinus and his disciple Porphyry, had transformed Plato's Greek philosophy into a more personal and religious perspective. In Neo-Platonism, Augustine discovered a belief in God as a spiritual reality rather than a superphysical entity. This appealed to Augustine. Yet he remained in despair because he could not find a genuine point of contact between humanity and the Neo-Platonists' highly spiritualized God.

Morally, Augustine could fare no better. He lamented over and over again that his life was controlled by his physical appetites and his inflated sense of self-importance. Often, in the *Confessions,* he spoke of his many sensual desires and his haughty delight in being intellectually superior to others. The lust and pride that consumed Augustine's life caused him to curve inward upon himself. Later, he was to call this sin. He seemed unable to escape from within the circle of his own preoccupations. He was quite literally an individual stuck on himself.

From our own experiences, we can recognize this brutal circle of entrapment. To always be fixed upon one's own ego is a wearisome way to live. Self-pleasure and self-satisfaction, if not held in check, can easily turn into self-loathing and lethargy. Eventually, there is no way out of the self—no exit. This is exactly what happened to Augustine.

In brief, the young Augustine had become extravagant and reckless (a prodigal) in his personal gratification and sense of self-importance. He tells us in the *Confessions* that without mounting a horse, or boarding a ship, or even taking a step, he had traveled to a distant country. He was far removed from his true self and what God intended him to be. The burning question for Augustine was how to break free from his closed circle of despair. With God's grace, the breakthrough came in Augustine's thirtieth year.

The Other

In the year 384, while he was in Milan, Augustine met Bishop Ambrose. Ambrose was different from anyone Augustine had known before. For the first time, Augustine met a Christian who was his intellectual equal and yet a person who was a faithful child of the church of Christ. He became the other in Augustine's life. Bishop Ambrose helped release this prodigal son from his self-imposed spiritual prison. Augustine writes in book 5 of the *Confessions:*

> So I came to Milan and to Bishop Ambrose, who was known throughout the world as one of the best of men. He was a devout worshiper of you, Lord, and at that time his energetic preaching provided your people with choicest wheat and the joy of oil and the sober intoxication of wine. Unknowingly I was led by you to him, so that through him I might be led, knowingly, to you.[7]

Augustine had found his role model—the one whose preaching and teaching he would emulate. But even more important, he had discovered the one who would lead him to God through the gospel of Christ.

It is a remarkable thing to find that other person in our experience who seems to change everything. It is a wonderful gift from God. And in turn, we by God's grace become that gift for others. In this manner, Augustine responded to Ambrose, and he became a useful vessel for God in return. Howard Thurman has written of this kind of redemptive relationship, "to be to another human being what is needed at the time that the need is most urgent and most acutely felt, this is to participate in the precise act of redemption."[8] Thus it was with Augustine and Ambrose.

Ambrose's preaching helped the prodigal Augustine over several key intellectual and spiritual hurdles. Augustine had been in that distant country of Jesus' parable, and now in his own assessment he was beginning to come home. Ambrose, ever the sophisticated Roman, used the best of Neo-Platonism and the classics of Greco-Roman literature to serve the Christian gospel. He helped Augustine understand how God is spirit and not material; he aided Augustine in comprehending that evil, although quite real, does not have an independent existence but rather is the direct result of the absence of good. Ambrose's God was capable of embracing all reality, while not being limited by any part of it. This way of understanding God and the world greatly appealed to Augustine.

Even more important, through Ambrose, the reticent Augustine was able to appreciate and enjoy Christian worship for the first time. In Ambrose's inspired preaching and through his innovative use of music, Augustine began to see that the mystical dimension of life could enhance rational discourse rather than contradict it. In the mystery of the Eucharist (communion), Augustine discovered the presence of a mediator between God and humanity. He was coming closer and closer to Jesus Christ.

The Bible and the Garden

One obstacle remained to Augustine's conversion—the Bible itself. Although Monica had instructed her son in God's Word from an early age, Augustine failed to find anything compelling in its pages and thought of many of its passages as "absurd" and filled with "crude opinions" (*Confessions,* book 6). But again, it was Bishop Ambrose who changed Augustine's thinking.

In his preaching, Ambrose used the Bible in a new way for Augustine. He recalls in book 6 of the *Confessions,* "I heard some difficult passages of the Old Testament explained figuratively; such passages had been death to me because I was taking them literally." Augustine learned from Ambrose to seek for the deeper meaning of a biblical text. Although the precise allegorical method applied by Ambrose and Augustine might strike us at times as fanciful, it liberated him from a wooden, literal translation that allowed for only one meaning in the text.

The essential point was that Augustine was freed by Ambrose's approach to Scripture to apply his own intellect to the Bible. It began to speak to him in new and exciting ways. Augustine never forgot Ambrose's encouragement about an open and free study of the Scriptures. In book 6 of the Confessions, Augustine reports, "I delighted to hear Ambrose often asserting in his sermons to the people, as a principle on which he must insist emphatically, *The letter is death-dealing, but the spirit gives life.*" Augustine began reading the Bible in this new light.

With this lead, Augustine soon unearthed some of Scripture's richest treasures. We know how central Jesus' parable of the prodigal son was for Augustine's faith journey, but he also fell in love with the psalms. His *Confessions* are laced with references from the psalms, most of which he wrote from memory. In fact, much like the psalms of the Old Testament, Augustine's *Confessions* are addressed directly to God—and like the psalmist, he looks deeply into his own character, passing judgment upon himself as he seeks divine mercy.

However, it was Paul's writings in the New Testament that finally convinced Augustine of his self-centeredness and sin and of his need to turn toward God and be converted. In book 7 of the *Confessions,* he professes, "I seized on the hallowed calligraphy of your spirit [the Bible], and most especially the writings of the apostle Paul." Previously Augustine had viewed Paul's work as self-contradictory, but now he experienced it as "a single face to me."

Through Paul, Augustine discovered that the gospel of God is all about grace. But this unmerited gift of divine love cannot be received until the heart is humbled. This was the difficult last hurdle for Augustine, as it is for so many of us. He had to let go of his success-driven life in the Roman world; he had to give up his reckless pursuit of personal pleasure; and he had to admit that he could not save himself. Once he confessed his need, the way was open for his dramatic conversion. Augustine writes in the *Confessions:*

> So I began to read, and discovered that every truth I had read in those other books was taught here [in the Bible] also, but now inseparably from your gift of grace, so that no one who sees can boast as though what he sees and the very power to see it were not from you—for who has anything that he had not received?[9]

Augustine had finally turned the corner to come home. Paul's writing on grace helped him to realize that during his time of searching for God, God had been searching for him. Even when he had been most distant from God in his prodigal journey, God's grace in Jesus Christ was ever present—if only he had had eyes to see and ears to hear. The kingdom of God was always there in his midst.

Intellectually convinced about the truth of the gospel and convinced of his need to permit God into his life, Augustine still held back from becoming a Christian. As he did with so much else, he continued to struggle internally for greater clarity and insight. By this point in reading the *Confessions,* we wonder if the hesitant saint will ever let go of his tortured ego.

Then it happened! In a garden outside his villa, Augustine gave in to God. The pressure of his internal turmoil had become emotionally unbearable, when suddenly he heard something like a child's voice at play singing repeatedly, "Pick it up and read, pick it up and read." But there were no children playing nearby; there was no music being sung; there was only the inexplicable voice of God. In response, the prodigal son of Monica picked up "the book of the apostle's letters" and at random read and translated these words from St. Paul: "Not in dissipation and drunkenness, nor in debauchery and lewdness, nor in arguing and jealousy; but put on the Lord Jesus Christ, and make no provision for the flesh or gratification of your desires" (Romans 13:13–14).

Augustine need read no further. He wrote in book 8 of the *Confessions:* "No sooner had I reached the end of the verse than the light of certainty flooded my heart and all dark shades of doubt fled away." After so many years in the distant country as a prodigal son, his heart and mind had now been transformed—he had received the gift of faith.

What are we to make of this kind of emotional conversion? Blindly opening the Bible to a random page for inspiration, after hearing a voice, is not the usual recommended method for responsible Bible study. Yet, for the highly intellectual Augustine and his overexercised rationality, perhaps God had little other choice. For the headstrong Augustine, there may have been no other way—the "light of certainty" needed to flood his heart so that "all dark shades of doubt fled away." In the end, just as the biblical prodigal son had given up his carefully prepared speech in lieu of his father's loving embrace, so too Augustine, the great teacher of rhetoric, fell silent so that God's overwhelming grace might speak to him.

Faith and Convalescence

The homecoming of the prodigal Augustine to faith did not mean that the remainder of his journey was to be smooth. The great surprise of the *Confessions* is that at the time of its writing, the forty-three-year-old Augustine, now a bishop, still struggled with his many temptations. Because of this, he pictured himself as a convalescing patient in his spiritual life rather than as a cured soul. This frank admission of his struggles may have shocked many of his contemporary readers. Much like the unexpected twists and turns of Jesus' parables, the good bishop's insistence that he continued to be a sinner, and not a saint, jolted his readers.

In book 10 of the *Confessions,* Augustine looked back with deep appreciation for his conversion experience a decade before: "You pierced my heart with your word, and I fell in love with you." But the joyous convert, like so many of us, was painfully aware of what a slow process transformation into a new life in Christ can be.

From his past, Augustine regretted many things. He lamented his harsh dismissal of the woman he had lived with for fourteen years. This he had done just prior to his conversion. As theologian Margaret Miles points out, Augustine could not even bring himself to name her in the *Confessions*.[10] She remains a faceless entity in history, even though this common-law wife would have known and loved Augustine more deeply than did his closest friends. We can only wonder how much more complete Augustine's understanding of grace might have been if he had opened himself to learn more from the caring mother of his only child.

Augustine was painfully aware that he was still a work in progress. Maria Boulding writes of Augustine, "He gives a picture of conversion as a continuous, slow, and sometimes painful process, rather than dramatic once-for-all."[11] Thus, a decade after his experience of conversion, Augustine not only has regrets about his past but also recognizes the daily temptations of the present. His pride of knowledge and his sensual desires remained constant companions.

In the end, Augustine teaches us that Christ, the great physician, continues to tend to our convalescing souls. Perhaps none of us are cured souls. But like Augustine, we are on our way to health. Or, in the language of Jesus' parable, we are all prodigals constantly in the process of coming home. We have been in the distant country far from God. Like Augustine, we may be both the younger and older brothers of the parable—at times excessive and reckless in our own self-centeredness, at other times extravagant in our self-righteousness.

Yet, also like Augustine, we are recipients of God's excessive love. With Jesus' help, we catch a glimpse of the kingdom of God in our midst—compassion without end. And like all prodigals, we confess with the ancient Augustine, "you have made us for yourself, and our heart is restless until it rests in you."

CHAPTER THREE
Valley of the Shadow

Even though I walk through the darkest valley.
  I fear no evil;
for you are with me;
  your rod and your staff—
  they comfort me.

PSALM 23:4

No one ever told me that grief felt so like fear. I
am not afraid, but the sensation is like being afraid.
The same fluttering in the stomach, the same rest-
lessness, the yearning. I keep on swallowing. . . .
I dread the moments when the house is empty.

C. S. LEWIS, *A Grief Observed*

NO ONE ESCAPES DEATH. Both the ancient psalmist and the modern
Christian writer C. S. Lewis knew that death is faith's ultimate challenge. They understood the need to face up to death no matter how
difficult. They knew, almost instinctively, that how we confront death
bears directly on how we live—a theology of life is incomplete and inad-
equate when the topic of death is avoided or denied. For as the psalmist
and Lewis teach us, only within the valley of the shadow can life's greatest challenges be met.

Our Common Humanity

The psalms of the Hebrew Bible are about living and dying. Indeed,
they cover the whole range of human experience from birth to death.
According to Walter Brueggemann, reading the psalms is like hearing
"the voice of our own common humanity."[1] They speak for you and me:

sometimes they are filled with praise, and life is wonderful; sometimes they are heavy with lament, and life is bleak. At times they are generous and forgiving, at other times they are petty and vindictive. We are the Bible's 150 psalms. Like them, we know the roller-coaster ride of life.

For example, in Psalm 22, the psalmist covers the range of human emotion from lament to praise. In this psalm, traditionally ascribed to King David, the ancient poet begins with a lament—broken and utterly forsaken. But by the psalm's conclusion, the writer has risen to a tremendous affirmation and praise of God. It causes us to wonder: What is our true condition as human beings? Are we broken and near defeat? Are we beaten down by life? Or are we triumphant and joyous— counting the many blessings of God? The answer in the psalms is that we are both; lament and praise are equally relevant when life is embraced realistically. In this sense, the psalms are neither optimistic nor pessimistic: they are realistic. They are honest to God about life and death and everything in between.

Psalm 23

In the famous Twenty-third Psalm, another of David's psalms, this ancient hero of Israel faced death squarely. But this psalm is so familiar to us that we must be careful in its interpretation. There is great danger in taking the psalm for granted. My experience is a case in point. Ever since childhood, Psalm 23 has provided a comforting framework for my evening prayers. Between the opening, "The Lord is my shepherd," and the closing, "I shall dwell in the house of the LORD forever," I have discovered great comfort—and still do.

However, David's remarkable statement that he will "fear no evil" as he walks "through the valley of the shadow of death" requires closer scrutiny. On what basis can he make this claim? His confidence was not in his moral reputation. Although David had been a man after God's own heart, he also had committed adultery and murder. In his affair with Bathsheba, David as king had set himself above the laws of God and had taken a married woman for himself. My hero, and Israel's hero, had clay feet. He was a flawed individual. In fact, David committed one sin upon another by having Uriah, Bathsheba's husband, killed in battle. Found out by his court prophet Nathan, David had to repent before God and the nation. He was more of a sinner than a saint. His deeds of heroism for Israel were great; his sins were even greater.

Surely David's courage in the face of death could not be based on his own virtue or moral veracity. My childhood image of the heroic David at prayer required adjustment given the realities of David's life. Where does his courage in the face of death come from? We need to look beyond his or our vices and virtues for an answer.

Death in the Psalms

If David's courage in facing death did not result from his own moral fitness, could it be derived from his Hebraic view of an afterlife? Here again, the answer would have to be no. As C. S. Lewis reminds us, "It seems quite clear that in most parts of the Old Testament there is little or no belief in a future life; certainly no belief that is of any religious importance."[2] This assessment is shared by most biblical scholars. It is true that the word *soul* often appears in English translations of the Hebrew *ruach* in the psalms, but it means something more like "life" and doesn't presuppose immortality or any meaningful survival past the grave. Therefore, David did not have a general notion of immortality to fall back upon.

There is, of course, the land of the dead referred to in the psalms. This "Sheol" (in Hebrew) is merely a shadowy form of existence beyond death for good and bad alike. It is no more than a dim repository for things once human; it suggests no hope for any type of quality existence after death. The concept of the resurrection of the dead, with which many of us are familiar, represents a later development in Old Testament literature. It would not have been available to David's generation.

On the more positive side, David could think of survival beyond the grave in terms of his descendants. Indeed, the ancient people of Israel recognized that their future was in their children. We still find great strength in this notion, but this is not the same as individual survival of the self beyond this life. Yet David persisted. He believed that he would walk through the valley of death with God as his companion. The question remains: Where could David find a faith adequate for death's challenge? In what sense could he imagine God as his steady companion?

Imagination and Trust

Common agreement exists that the psalms were used in worship settings by ancient Israel. This would have been true of temple worship at Jerusalem before and after the time of the Babylonian captivity. Yet there is little agreement among scholars how the psalms may have been used in worship. They may have been sung as a regular part of the liturgy or perhaps used on special occasions during Israel's ancient calendar. We don't know for sure.

However, there is scholarly consensus that the psalms were written by poets—the result of inspired imagination. For example, Lewis is convinced that we miss the true impact of the psalms, including their views on death, if we fail to appreciate their poetic power. In *Reflections on the Psalms,* Lewis has written:

> Most emphatically the Psalms must be read as poems; as lyrics, with all the licenses and all the formalities, the hyperboles, the emotional rather than the logical connections, which are proper to lyric poetry.[3]

Many theologians agree that in order to grasp the spiritual power of the psalms, we must open ourselves to "the emotional rather than the logical connections." This was the intent of the ancient poets of Israel.

When David confronted the reality of death, as he does in Psalm 23, he is not doing so as an abstract exercise. He had many enemies as Israel's king. Death's dark valley was a real and present danger. He was undoubtedly protected by a royal guard, yet he also knew that death comes to us all—rich or poor, slave or free. Death, in the final analysis, is the poet's concern, not the politician's. And it was David as poet who had to deal with death. Politics and statecraft have no ultimate answers. If there were to be answers for this issue, they rested in the imagination of the poet. This is what makes the psalms so valuable for us—the poetic imagination can reach beyond time and space. The ways of the political and the cultural hero are earthbound, but not those of the poet. When David wrote, "Even though I walk through the darkest valley, I fear no evil; for you are with me," it was the poet speaking.

Death's great mysteries are confronted with imagination and antici-patory experience. We have not yet died, what can we expect? What do the psalms suggest?

Biblical scholar Thomas G. Long helps us at this point. He writes: "Psalms operate at the level of imagination, often swiveling the universe on the hinges of a single image."[4] In the darkest valley, David has nowhere else to turn but toward that "single image," the Lord God of Israel. With the single image of God introduced into the equation of life and death, David found his source of courage. He will not fear evil because God is with him. This alone makes the difference. For David, walking through the valley of the shadow is now possible because of his awareness of God's mysterious presence. As another psalmist indicates in Psalm 139, "If I ascend to heaven, you are there; if I make my bed in Sheol, you are there" (Psalm 139:8). Just as God is present throughout life, God will also be present through death. This has nothing to do with our virtues and vices. It does not concern any preconceived notions of personal immortality. David's courageous affirmation is based on only one reality, one image, the God who will not let us go.

David places his full trust in God. He does this because he believes God to be truly God. For David, and the psalms, death remains uncharted territory—there is no knowledge of what comes next, if anything. As in life so in death, he is totally dependent upon God for ultimate goodness and mercy. He does not know, but God does. It is this great mystery that follows David and us to death and beyond.

In facing life and death in the psalms, it is a matter of putting first things first. Again, borrowing from Lewis's *Reflections on the Psalms,* the point is that we are to center our faith in God. Then, and only then, do other matters like heaven and hell find their proper context and priority—heaven meaning communion with God and hell designating separation from God. All other discussion remains secondary. In Lewis's view

> Most of us find that our belief in the future life is strong only when God is in the centre of our thoughts; that if we try to use the hope of "Heaven" as a compensation (even for the most innocent and natural misery, that of bereavement) it crumbles away.[5]

The psalms agree. Placing God at the center is primary. All else is secondary, including our own restless desire to find heaven's gate.

C. S. Lewis (1898–1963)

It has been difficult to keep C. S. Lewis out of our discussions of the psalms since he is such a wonderful and provocative guide to their meaning for our lives. Like the ancient poets of Israel, he too sought to center his life in God—to put first things first. Perhaps this accounts for why this British writer, known to his friends as Jack, has touched the hearts and minds of millions of readers in the twentieth century. In a time so adrift spiritually and intellectually, Lewis offered a clarion call to return God to center stage in both public and private discourse. He believed only then could modern men and women begin to discern the great issues of life and death. As a teacher, scholar, literary critic, and churchman, he placed all his intellectual skills and writing talents in the service of God.

The psalms themselves were never far from Lewis's consciousness. From the time of his conversion to Christianity at the age of thirty-three in 1931, until his death in 1963, this professor of medieval and Renaissance literature at Oxford and Cambridge universities lived with the psalms. He recited them almost daily in his schools' chapel services and within his parish church on Sundays. The psalms acted as a sustaining spiritual guide and contributed many insights within his writings.

Author of more than thirty books, including well-known works like *The Screwtape Letters, The Chronicles of Narnia,* and *Mere Christianity,* Lewis addressed the challenges of being a Christian in the modern world. In doing so, he attacked a modern, materialistic worldview that he felt left little room for the exercise of theological imagination. He argued it is impossible to grasp the holy presence of God in a world that by definition has ruled out wonder and mystery. The presence of God as witnessed to by the psalms (or the Gospels for that matter) seems to elude the one-dimensional view of modern secularism. Using both reason and creative imagination, Lewis became the twentieth century's greatest popularizer of Christianity and its chief apologist in the English-speaking world. Applying rational argumentation, he pleaded with his reading public to open its imagination to realities much larger than the linear and box-like existence of modernity. The worlds in which modern men and women generally lived were much too small for Lewis. Even the vast perspective of most scientists and philosophers were flawed by an inability to appreciate imagination as well as rationality.

Lewis believed the modern Western world is trapped within its own secular assumptions. Its relativity of ideas and values ironically represent an absolutist rejection of the possibility of God's existence. In turn, Lewis's arguments for his belief in God, the supernatural, miracles, and the incarnation of Jesus Christ were judged to be antiquated and oversimplified by many philosophers and theologians. But the so-called common people flocked to his writings. Through his Christian apologetics, his children's stories, his science fiction, and his literary criticism, he spoke to a vast and varied array of readers in England and America.

On both sides of the Atlantic, as professional theologians and clerics offered mixed reviews, Lewis's books grew in popularity throughout his lifetime. This phenomenon only increased in the decades after his death. By 1980 worldwide sales of his books, now in scores of languages, numbered between 1 and 2 million copies annually. There are more than 40 million of his books in print. All this suggests that Lewis knew how to speak to issues that mattered to his readers. He got to where people lived.

Lewis and Death

Lewis knew that people thought much more often about death than they normally admitted. His experience of Britain's bombing by Germany during World War II convinced him of the need for a faith that could speak directly to issues of life and death. After the war, writing in *Reflections on the Psalms,* Lewis noted that whatever death might mean, God must mean more. He was convinced that the living God walks with us through the valley of death as the psalmist had indicated. This, for Lewis, was far more important than anything else that might be said about death. But how to convey this?

In *Surprised by Joy,* Lewis's account of events leading to his conversion to Christianity, there is a passage about death and the afterlife that on the surface may appear odd. Referring to his journey from atheism to Christianity, Lewis wrote:

> My conversion involved as yet no belief in a future life. I now number it among my greatest mercies that I was permitted for several months, perhaps for a year, to know God and to attempt obedience without even raising that question. My training was like that of the Jews, to whom He revealed Himself centuries before there was a whisper of anything better (or worse) beyond the grave than shadowy and featureless *Sheol*. And I did not dream even of that.[6]

Lewis's lack of belief in an afterlife immediately following his conversion allowed him to put first things first. Obedience to God, in Lewis's thought, should not be buttressed by the possibility of future rewards or punishments. God is to be obeyed and loved for no other reason than that God is God. We can almost hear the echo of the psalmist's voice against the distant hills.

Lewis, the new convert, understood what so many Christians forget: God is God and merits our commitment whether there be an afterlife or not. In fact, Lewis observed in the same passage, "I have never seen how a preoccupation with that subject [immortality] at the outset could fail to corrupt the whole thing."[7] He continued, "I had been brought up to believe that goodness was goodness only if it were disinterested, and that any hope of reward or fear of punishment contaminated the will."[8] Why should it be otherwise in ultimate matters like our relationship with God? In Lewis's plain reason, "God was to be obeyed simply because he was God."[9] For men and women of faith, courage to walk through the valley of the shadow was not derived from holding a trump card like an assurance of immortality but from merely trusting in God. For Christian belief, Christ's resurrection portends the resurrection of the believer, but the truth remains that even Jesus himself had "to walk that lonesome valley."

Like the psalmist, Lewis had realized the proper order of things—first God, then the rest. But as we shall see, that order itself was tested in ways Lewis himself could never have anticipated. Ironically, at the time he penned his *Reflections on the Psalms,* Lewis was moving from a consideration of death in general to death as a personal tragedy. He was about to face the painful death of his beloved wife, Joy Davidman.

A Grief Observed

When death comes, everything is rethought by the survivors. Death's sting means adjustments, reassessments, changes. Lewis had known loss before: his mother's death when he was nine years old and the death of friends in bloody trenches of France during the Great War had familiarized him with death's strong grip. He and thousands of others had faced the relentless Nazi bombings of London. But the pain of death was never so great as when late in life Lewis lost his wife of only four years to cancer.

In a most unlikely series of events, Lewis, a confirmed bachelor, married his friend Joy Davidman Gresham, a divorced American poet and writer. He did so in a civil ceremony on April 23, 1956, in order that Joy might become a British citizen. This allowed Joy to avoid deportation from her newfound life in England. Shortly thereafter, Joy was diagnosed with cancer and received a bleak prognosis. Then, in a bedside marriage, during December 1956, at Wingfield Hospital near Oxford, Lewis married Joy again in a Christian ceremony according to the rites of the Anglican church.[10]

Joy Davidman and Jack Lewis were very much in love. What had begun as friendship had blossomed into deep mutual love in every sense of the word. In yet another surprise, totally unexpected, rather than die during the course of 1958, Joy had an extraordinary recovery from her terminal bout with cancer. It was a miracle: no other explanations sufficed.

A key to understanding the love shared by Davidman and Lewis can be found in a series of radio talks on *The Four Loves* taped by Lewis in London during 1958. (These addresses were later published in book form under the same title.) According to Colin Duriez, the four kinds of love Lewis identified for his radio audience as affection, friendship, eros, and charity *(agape)* are precisely those evident in "the period of his [Lewis's] short but happy marriage to Joy Davidman."[11] True to Lewis's own experience; affection, friendship, and eros all contributed to the "gift-love" of charity, or divine love, in which he and Joy so fully shared. Jack had confided in his friend Neville Cayhill, "I never thought I would have in my sixties the happiness that passed me by in my twenties."[12] In Joy's love for Jack, he experienced the grace of God firsthand—completely and fully.

In 1960 Joy Davidman's cancer returned with a vengeance. This time there were to be no miracles, no delay of the dark valley. On July 13, at the age of forty-five, Joy died. Jack Lewis was devastated: the love that had been granted him so late in life was now suddenly taken from him. He felt the deep, deep lament of the psalmist. Life was brokenness.

What kind of a cruel joke was this? In his grief, Lewis shook his fist at God, even accusing God of being "The Cosmic Sadist, the spiteful imbecile."[13] In his anger and profound sense of loss, Lewis laid out all his feelings before God. Again, reminiscent of the psalms of ancient Israel, he articulated the voice of our common humanity. How can this be? Haven't I suffered enough, what more do you want from me? Just leave me alone. Lamentation.

Long before Lewis had met Davidman, he had published *The Problem of Pain* (1940), a book intended to "solve the intellectual problem raised by suffering."[14] But as for the reality of suffering itself, he wrote that he had nothing to offer his readers "except my conviction that when pain is to be borne, a little courage helps more than much knowledge, a little human sympathy more than much courage, and the least tincture of the love of God more than all."[15] In another wistful passage, Lewis referred to pain as God's megaphone. He claimed: "God whispers to us in our pleasures, speaks in our conscience, but shouts in our pains: it is His megaphone to rouse a deaf world."[16]

With Joy's death, however, none of these previous theological musings were sufficient for his present grief. He was walking through the valley of the shadow as never before. In addition to the pain of Joy's suffering and death, Jack himself had developed osteoporosis. He wrote to a friend during Joy's period of remission:

> Did I tell you I also have a bone disease? It is neither mortal nor curable: a prematurely senile loss of calcium. I was very crippled and had much pain all summer but am in a good spell now. I was losing calcium just about as fast as Joy was gaining it, and a bargain (if it were one) for which I'm very thankful.[17]

Lewis was engrossed in the death and dying of his beloved Joy. He related his medical problems in a substitutionary way to her suffering. He hoped against hope for her recovery. If only God would take him and not her. Thus, when the end came, there was no consoling Jack. In fact, the only relief he could find was similar to that of the ancient psalmist—he took up the pen in lament. During the first months after Joy's death, he kept a journal of his grief in unused notebooks he found around his home at the Kilns.

With blunt honesty, Lewis described his loss. In fewer than one hundred pages, he worked through his grief, finally restoring God to the center of his shattered life. However, what Lewis reports is anything but a "triumphant story" of an easy return to grace. His account is arduous and painful—in a word, real. It is brutally honest.

Later, Lewis permitted his reflections to be published. But he wrote under the pseudonym of N. W. Clerk to protect Joy's privacy (referred to as H), and to insure that his work be accepted on its own merits and not because it was written by the famous C. S. Lewis. Only after his death was it revealed that *A Grief Observed* was written by this great Christian author.

Interestingly, *A Grief Observed* has received mixed reviews from Lewis's admirers. Some think it is too raw a literary product and too filled with doubts for a true representation of Lewis and his theology. But others, like me, find *A Grief Observed* to be Lewis's most inspiring work. Like the ancient psalmist, Lewis reports here exactly how he feels, not how he is supposed to feel. We are never closer to the real C. S. Lewis than in this masterful piece of writing. At the beginning of *A Grief Observed*, Lewis is vulnerable—and he knows it. "You never know," he writes, "how much you really believe anything until its truth or falsehood becomes a matter of life and death."[18] How many of us have not been there? Lewis's common humanity shines through, and he hurts in ways many of us can understand.

Friends tried to comfort Lewis, but he was not receptive. Efforts at sympathy are for the most part sincere. He appreciated that. Yet religious clichés in his time of grief were unacceptable to him. He lamented:

> Talk to me about the truth of religion and I'll listen gladly. Talk to me about the duty of religion and I'll listen submissively. But don't come talking to me about the consolations of religion or I shall suspect that you don't understand.[19]

Trite words about reunions on the other shore and facile sentiments about it being God's will struck the grieving Lewis as not genuine. He knew the Bible too well to accept simplistic pictures of cheerful angels sitting on clouds playing harps for all eternity. This was an evasion of death's harsh reality. It all rang false for Lewis.

The response of faith to death must somehow rise above trivial religious characterizations and pat theological rhetoric. For Lewis, it was time to get real, to be honest to God about death. "What chokes every prayer and every hope," he writes, "is the memory of all the prayers H. and I offered and all the false hope we had."[20] How cruel it seemed to

Lewis that God would grant a remission of the cancer, only to permit its torturous return.

Lewis took up the issues of his heart in a straightforward fashion with God. He cried out to God (like the psalmist, like Christ from the cross). What kind of God are you? Have you forsaken me? He knew that the real issue was not the question of God's existence; this he didn't doubt. The real problem, for Lewis, was that God might not be the loving and merciful God he thought God to be. Perhaps God was a cruel and heartless Power. Shaking his fist at God, Lewis put the Creator on trial—defend yourself, God!

At times during his grief, Lewis would become conscious of his passion and anger. He would then back off and reflect on his accusations against God: "I wrote that [Lewis's accusations] last night. It was a yell rather than a thought." Lewis continued, "Let me try it over again. Is it rational to believe in a bad God? Anyway, in a God so bad as all that? The Cosmic Sadist, the spiteful imbecile?"[21] Lewis knew in his more rational moments that he couldn't make God into the Universal Culprit responsible for everything that goes wrong. That would be as simplistic as those who would make God into a Cosmic Caretaker who meets our every need upon demand.

In sum, we find Lewis wrestling with God, struggling to endure the loss of Joy. "On the rebound," Lewis observes, "one passes into tears and pathos. Maudlin tears." This was difficult and embarrassing for Lewis. Like us, he did not want to be out of control. He adds, "I almost prefer the moments of agony. These are at least clean and honest."[22] Many things confused Lewis.

Lewis wondered how best to remember his wife and lover. What had become of Joy and his memory of Joy? His own words paint the picture best. Those who have loved and lost know them best.

> At first I was very afraid of going places where H. and I had been happy—our favorite pub, our favorite wood. But I decided to do it at once. . . . Unexpectedly, it makes no difference. Her absence is no more emphatic in those places than anywhere else. It's not local at all. . . . Her absence is like the sky, spread over everything.[23]

Lewis feared the loss of details about Joy's memory, a common feeling among those who grieve. He worries, "I have no photograph of her that's any good. I cannot even see her face distinctly in my imagination." How can this be? In irony Lewis observes, "yet the odd face of some stranger seen in a crowd this morning may come before me in vivid perfection the moment I close my eyes tonight." But what of his beloved Joy? Grief is so confusing. In one of the most poignant lines of

A Grief Observed, Lewis agonizes, "But her voice is still vivid. The remembered voice—that can turn me at any moment to a whimpering child."[24] Strange indeed are the things remembered and forgotten.

Lewis wondered if he would ever regain his equilibrium. How long would grief last? Would things ever be normal again? Would there come a dramatic moment at which there would be a movement away from grief? In fact, Lewis's first steps out of grief were mundane and unremarkable. It all began with a practical decision on his part. He would write no more about his grief and loss. Lewis had filled four notebooks with his thoughts. He wrote near the end of *A Grief Observed,* "This is the fourth—and last—empty MS. book I can find in the house." Enough is enough. He concluded, "In so far as this record was a defense against total collapse, a safety valve, it has done some good."[25] But Lewis knew it was time to move on.

He had traveled through his grief, not by denying loss or by repressing pain but by courageously embracing it all. Like the ancient psalmist, he cried out to God and tried to make the best of it he could. Gradually Lewis began to notice a subtle shift in his daily life as he relocated his spiritual center once again in God. "Yea, though I walk through the valley of the shadow of death, I will fear no evil: for thou art with me" (Psalm 23:4, KJV). Lewis's emphasis had shifted from the first clause to the second. God was once again being given the primacy.

Turning Back to Life

The fourth and final section of *A Grief Observed* is more like a beginning than an ending. Perhaps a fresh start, or maybe even better, a return to the center describes best what happened to Lewis. In this last section, Lewis's voice is fuller and its tone is much more luminous. After all his emotional and intellectual dislocation, Lewis had returned to the spiritual center that had sustained and enriched his life for so long. He was once again at peace with God.

It was not exactly the same C. S. Lewis as before. Death changes us all. Lewis's confidence had been shaken, but he was far more human now. He knew now with his heart what he had once known only with his head—thou art with me. Lewis had walked (literally limped) through the valley of the shadow, and he had been thrown off his spiritual path.

In his grief, Lewis had lost sight of the theological principle so dear to him and the psalmist—first things first. He confessed in section 4 of *A Grief Observed,* "The notes have been about myself, and about H., and about God. In that order." But he had gotten things backwards.

This is what personal grief and loss can do to us. Our whole perspective goes haywire. It is very hard at these times to get outside ourselves. We are grounded in our responses. How else can it be with such shock? Lewis said, however, that the order of his thoughts was exactly "what they ought not to have been."[26] Through his writing (after three note-books), he finally saw the significance of his upside-down approach. He had valued everything in terms of how it affected him. Reversing the order, he gained a fresh perspective—actually, it was his old spiritual perspective renewed in light of his present experiences.

Beginning again with God, Lewis rediscovered that praise and thanksgiving is a mode of love that always has some element of joy within it, regardless of the circumstances. In his case, it meant praise of God as the giver of all that he had experienced, especially thanksgiving for Joy herself as God's great gift to him. In all her strengths and weaknesses, she had blessed Lewis's life. She had helped Lewis to discover his full humanity.

As for himself, Lewis recognized the great temptation to idolatry within his ego-centered grief. He had almost made a god out of his own sorrow. However, God once again proved to be the great iconoclast for Lewis. Former images of his grief began to shatter, and his self-made monument to Joy as the center of his grief was also broken. Lewis realized that even his relationship with God had been wholly consumed by grief. His response to death had narrowed his entire outlook on life to himself and how everything affected him.

But now Lewis was back on course. He still didn't have all the answers for why everything happened the way it did. Yet he knew in his heart that God, then Joy, then himself, was the proper order of things. And so he moved from the egocentrism of his early grief back to the theocentrism that had marked his maturing years, including his intimate and glorious relationship with Joy. Whatever came next, this much Lewis trusted for certain: First things must come first—even in the valley of the shadow. The psalmist must have smiled knowingly!

CHAPTER FOUR

Deep River

O LORD, you have searched me and know me.
You know when I sit down and when I rise up;
   you discern my thoughts from far away.
You search out my path and my lying down,
   and are acquainted with all my ways.
Even before a word is on my tongue,
   O LORD, you know it completely.
You hem me in, behind and before,
   and lay your hand upon me.
Such knowledge is too wonderful for me;
   it is so high that I cannot attain it.

PSALM 139:1–6

The Lord is!
   He is more than tongue can tell,
   Than mind can think, than heart can feel!
The Lord is my strength.
   When day is done and in weariness I lay
     me down to sleep,
   When fear becomes a lump in my throat
     and an illness in my stomach,
   When the waters of temptation engulf me
     and I strangle beneath the waves,
   When I have thought myself empty and
     the solution to my problem hides, . . .
   When the tidings are of brooding clouds of war
     and of marching feet and humming planes
     moving in the awful rhythm of the dirge of death—
The Lord is the strength of my life.
   Of whom
     and what
       shall I be afraid?

HOWARD THURMAN, *Deep Is the Hunger*

THE LORD IS! This kind of bold faith expressed by Psalm 139 and Howard Thurman acknowledges a God whose reality and presence permeates all of life. God is far beyond our limited powers to comprehend, and yet somehow we know of the Creator because we are known. Such knowledge is too wonderful! According to the psalmist, God does indeed understand us: the Lord God has searched us and has discerned our thoughts from afar. Because we are known, we are able to know the unknowable.

Like the psalmist, Howard Thurman believes we can know the unknowable. Being known by God, and knowing God, grants a pathway for the psalmist and Thurman into the heart of God—the goal and source of life itself. Both the ancient poet and this modern mystic find an opening to deep faith, to the primary experience of God.

In what follows, we will explore together the encounter with God expressed in Psalm 139 and the writings of Howard Thurman, the grandson of an African American slave. We will try to understand how such an encounter can, in the idiom of Howard Thurman, bend our question marks into exclamation points. For this is the possibility of genuine faith!

Psalm 139

The key word in Psalm 139 is "know." It appears in several forms in verses 1, 2, 4, 6, and 14; and twice in verse 23. In all but one of these cases (verse 14), the "knowing" referred to is that of God's knowledge of us. As in Francis Thompson's well-known poem "The Hound of Heaven," God is pictured by the psalmist as the One who seeks us out, pursues us, and searches our hearts. Even before we have a conscious awareness of the Divine, we are already known by our Maker. This is the Reality that Howard Thurman referred to in the opening quotation of our chapter as "the strength of my life." The use of the word "know" exactly seven times in Psalm 139 is more than coincidental.

J. Clinton McCann Jr., writing in the *New Interpreter's Bible,* tells us that the number seven signifies fullness or completeness for the ancient Hebrew. The psalmist is indicating to the reader that we are fully and completely known by God.[1] This was indeed good news for those who first heard these words some five hundred years before Jesus' birth. According to biblical scholar Bernhard W. Anderson, the entire book of the psalms in its present form is a product of the postexilic community of Israel. It is in essence the "hymnbook of the second temple."[2] Returning from captivity in Babylon, the people and leaders of Jerusalem who rebuilt their city and temple needed to know that God was with them. The psalmist provided them with this assurance. We too need to hear these redeeming words. And we can. As we learned in our study of the Twenty-third Psalm, these ancient poems of Israel are not time bound. In reference to Psalm 139, McCann has noted, "It has communicated good news to persons in all places and times."[3]

The central message of Psalm 139, that we are known by God, speaks to us across the centuries. Such knowledge *is* too wonderful! It signals to us our intrinsic worth and value as human beings. To be known by God means to never be alone, never isolated, never ignored. We have status and standing within life because each of us is known by the Creator of the universe. What a remarkable revelation!

Nothing is more devastating to our human psyche than nonrecognition. Not to be acknowledged by others, for whatever reason, is tantamount to being dead. Individuals and groups who are marginalized in our society (the poor, the handicapped, the disinherited because of race, gender, or sexual orientation) know what this is like. Even if we are not among our society's marginalized, we may nevertheless experience the sting of being ignored by a friend or a colleague. The words "pain" and "death" are not too strong for such experiences.

The psalmist, and the people of Judah, must have had this type of experience in Babylon, a foreign and hostile culture. The ancient poet, looking back on this experience, felt compelled to remind his people that they were still loved and known by God. They had not heard good news for many years. Someone needed to tell Israel they counted, that they were somebody. They had been nobodies long enough. In Howard Thurman's words, they were to be valued because we all are children of God.[4] This is an irreducible fact, regardless of how others might feel or act toward us.

However, the fifth verse of Psalm 139 may puzzle us in this regard. The psalmist declares: "you hem me in, behind and before, and lay your hand upon me." Could the good news of God's searching us out be too intense for us to handle? Could the idea of God hemming us in, behind and before, and laying a hand upon us, be too suffocating and oppressive? Has God stepped across the line and violated our space and freedom as human beings? I suppose the passage could be read with this emphasis.

But viewed from another angle, this kind of question begins to disappear. What if to be surrounded by God's presence, and to sense the Divine hand upon us, means something different? What if it means to discover a sense of security and well being we have lacked or have been denied? Given this interpretation, God's presence becomes a liberating experience that frees us. Rather than being bound we are set loose. In light of verse 6, the interpretation of verse 5 as liberation seems quite plausible. In verse 6, the psalmist says of God's pervasive Being: "such knowledge is too wonderful for me; it is so high that I cannot attain it." In this kind of joyous knowledge, God has anointed us and freed us, not chained us and enslaved us. The hand of God removes the constraints of life. It is in this context that Howard Thurman can proclaim, "of whom and what shall I be afraid?"

Thus far we have focused on the beginning verses of Psalm 139, but it is helpful as well to draw out the lines of the psalm's overall structure. Verses 1 through 6, as we have seen, celebrate the fact that God seeks us out and finds us. The question is then raised in verse 7 as to where we might go to escape from God's presence. The answer comes back in verses 8 through 12 that there is literally no place we can go to escape God's loving reach. God's geography knows no limits.

We are reminded once again of Jonah. He could not escape God, no matter how hard he tried. The Lord God pursued him wherever he fled. The psalmist makes this same point, but even more radically. In verse 8 the palmist says "if I make my bed in Sheol, you are there." At this point, Psalm 139 surpasses even the accepted theology of ancient Israel. The Hebrew people had defined Sheol as a shadowy form of afterlife devoid of God. But now, God descends even to Sheol in our pursuit. There are literally and figuratively no boundaries that God cannot cross in order to effect the possibility of our redemption, our reunion with the Creator.

Thus for the psalmist, not even the proverbial gates of hell can prevail against the Creator and Redeemer of life. What a remarkable God! Relentless in our pursuit. There is no corner of darkness that cannot be illuminated by the living God. This theme comes back to us again and again in our *lectio divina*. It is well worth our contemplation: "Where can I go from your spirit? Or where can I flee from your presence?" (Psalm 139:7). The amazing answer is nowhere—absolutely nowhere.

The remaining verses of Psalm 139 deserve more attention than we can give here. Verses 13 to 18 speak of our relation to the creative processes of God, while verses 19 to 24 express the psalmist's opposition and condemnation of those who oppose God. Sometimes this last section is omitted in modern contexts of worship and personal devotion because it calls for revenge against God's enemies. In loyalty to God, the psalmist condemns those deemed to be God's enemies. The psalmist himself appears to forget that judgment rests with God and not with him. Jesus reminded a later generation, "Do not judge, so that you may not be judged" (Matthew 7:1). Perhaps this is a corrective to the psalmist's eager desire to destroy all those he deems God's adversaries.

The psalmist's holy enthusiasm for instant judgment should make us more than a little uncomfortable in light of Jesus' words.

Yahweh and You

What really matters in Psalm 139 is the relationship between Yahweh (the Lord) and we humans, a relationship built upon knowing and being known. J. Clinton McCann Jr. emphasizes this point in his commentary on Psalm 139.

> The very first word of the psalm is the divine name "Yahweh," and the first word of v. 2 is the emphatic Hebrew pronoun "you." While vv. 1–6 are often described as a statement of God's omniscience, what really matters about God to the psalmist is that the divine "you" knows "me."[5]

The biblical encounter between God and human beings is described by the philosopher Martin Buber as an "I/Thou" relationship. It is intimate and highly personal. In this remarkable meeting, both God and humanity retain their identities as bona fide subjects. Neither is treated as a mere object. God is not simply an object of worship like some idol; and humans are not merely objects to be manipulated by some capricious god. Rather, the biblical God is a subject who seeks to enter into relationship with all creation—most especially with humanity. Likewise, we as subjects have the capacity to seek a free and empowering relationship with God.

In the "I/Thou" relationship, a mutual respect exists between God and humans. God is sovereign, but God has endowed us with true freedom. With this gift, we are able to choose for or against our Creator. That is what freedom means—genuine choice. But to make good choices, knowledge of ourselves, of our world, and of God is essential. Without the proper knowledge of each other on the human and divine level, there can be no genuine relationship. Notice, on four different occasions at the beginning of Psalm 139 the word *know* (in Hebrew, *yada*) is used to indicate the psalmist's desire to know and be known fully by God.[6] Knowing is given primary importance by the psalmist and thus is mentioned at the start of this masterful psalm.

The desire to know and be known helps to accentuate the personal nature of the Bible's divine-human encounter. For example, in Genesis 4:1, Adam is said to "know" Eve in the act of sexual intimacy and procreation. The same Hebrew term is repeated in Psalm 139, where the word *know (yada)* is used in reference to knowledge of God. The ancient Hebrews knew that on the human level no knowledge is more complete and yet mysterious than the "knowing" of sexual intimacy and commitment. From a biblical perspective, our relationship with God is no less personal and intimate.

Therefore, the relationship between God and the psalmist in Psalm 139 is quite positive. This ancient poet exhibited a deep trust that we can know and be known by God through relationship. This optimism, however, does not run throughout the entire Psalter. For example, the poet of Psalm 137, writing during the Babylonian exile, laments a lack of relationship with God during his time of national disaster and personal tragedy. "By the waters of Babylon," wrote this psalmist, "there we [the people of Judah] sat down and wept, when we remembered Zion [Jerusalem]." The covenant (relationship) seemed to have dissolved.

Things can and do turn sour in relationships. The ups and downs of the people of God, for example, is a matter of biblical record. But even the negative encounters of ancient Israel with their God had some remnant of meaning. The lamentation of Psalm 137 speaks of a situation that could not be celebrated. The suffering of the people would be dishonored and trivialized if we tried to place a positive spin on these events. But the maintenance of a fragile relationship with God, even when things had gone wrong, should not be overlooked. It represents a courageous act of faith—even if it means only to sit down and weep.

To remain in relationship with God, whether it is a positive or negative experience, is essential for biblical faith. Once the relationship is severed, all hope is lost. In this regard, writer Elie Wiesel argues that to be a Jew one can be for God or against God but never without God.[7] This is the reality of biblical experience. For the ancient people of Israel, it was possible to love God or be estranged from God. In either case, the relationship still existed. After all, to care enough to shake your fist at the Creator assumes a relationship—albeit a strained relationship. But to show indifference toward God indicates that the relationship has been ended and is dead. This is the awful death of God in our hearts.

It is not an option for biblical people to be indifferent to God. To be so would be like showing indifference to life itself. It is true that human relationships can become so hurtful that they must be dissolved, but the same cannot apply to God if faith is to live. According to Howard Thurman, cutting ourselves off from God separates us from the goal and source of life itself. Psalm 139 reminds us that such actions lead to death rather than life. From this point of view, the opposite of faith is not doubt but indifference. Our doubts are not the real issue here. After all, God has searched us and knows us very well (Psalm 139:1). Nothing about us can shock God. In fact, our questions and doubts can be a dynamic part of our faith as they are encompassed by God's love. God embraces us—doubts and all.

However, we are in serious jeopardy when we are apathetic to God. When we stop asking questions in our faith, when we become indifferent to life, when we close ourselves off from God, we are dangerously close to unfaith. Without being attentive to God, darkness spreads across our troubled lives, and we are eclipsed in the shadows of our own indifference.

But in relationship with God, even the darkness is as light according to the psalmist. We may still have our doubts and uncertainties, our pains and sorrows, and like the ancient poet, we may cry out, "surely the darkness shall cover me, and the light around me become as night" (Psalm 139:11). However, also like the psalmist, we know that darkness is not the final word. For as we discover in the next verse: "even the darkness is not dark to you; the night is as bright as the day, for darkness is as light to you" (Psalm 139:12).

Our relationship with God, whether positive or negative, is the beginning of genuine life. Without it, we are lost, adrift without true direction. We are without a spiritual north on our compass. To know and be known is what it is all about for Psalm 139. With such knowledge "too wonderful" for words, we can live an abundant life, far beyond anything we ever could have expected or imagined.

Other Times, Other Places

The wisdom of faith found in the psalms did not escape the notice of early Christians. The New Testament quotes from the psalms more frequently than from any other book in the Hebrew Scriptures (Old Testament). The early followers of Jesus drew upon the psalms for their worship and prayers. They recognized the theological relevance of the psalmist's account of the divine-human encounter for their own experience of the risen Christ. According to J. Clinton McCann Jr., "the perspective of the psalter [from beginning to end] is pervasively eschatological [forward looking]; it affirms God's claim on the world . . . and on every individual life."[8] It speaks of the meeting between God and humanity.

Christian claims to meet God in Jesus Christ were a logical extension of the psalmist's message of encounter. The psalmist, so the Christian reasoned, knew of God's age-old desire to fulfill and complete the divine-human encounter, to bring together God and humanity in an I/Thou relationship. This was accomplished for Christians with Jesus Christ being the Way to a lasting encounter—once and for all.

The apostle Paul makes this theological connection when he declares that nothing in heaven or on earth can separate us from the love of God in Christ Jesus. That is to say, God's endless efforts to be in fellowship, or relationship, with humanity are now assured. Along these lines, McCann has observed: "While obviously not appropriating the message through Jesus Christ as Paul was, the psalmist knew essentially the same good news about God."[9] God will not be denied—God's love for humans cannot ultimately be rebuffed.

Thus the psalmist's faith that we can know and be known by God stretched far beyond ancient Israel. It reached into other times and other places. It extended to the divine-human encounter of Jesus Christ that his followers experienced throughout the ancient Mediterranean world. But why stop there? If we are to believe Psalm 139, God seeks us out in every age and in every place. The psalmist's confidence that we shall know God, as we are known, is a message as timely today as it was when it was first proclaimed. No individual has grasped the significance of this good news more completely than Howard Thurman, our dialog partner for reflections on Psalm 139.

Howard Thurman (1899–1981)

Howard Thurman, according to the jacket cover of his autobiography, was "a black minister, philosopher, and educator whose vitality and vision touched the lives of countless peoples of all races, faiths, and cultures."[10] Dr. Thurman is perhaps best known as the cofounder and pastor of the first multiracial, multicultural church in the United States, the Church for the Fellowship of All Peoples, established in San Francisco in 1944. He also made his reputation as the dean of the chapel at Howard University and Boston University. While at Boston he became the first African American to hold a full-time faculty appointment at that prestigious international university.

At midcentury *Life* magazine recognized Howard Thurman as one of the twelve greatest preachers in modern American life. His friendship with Martin Luther King Jr. and Mahatma Gandhi placed him in historic company. Writing in *Ebony* magazine in 1978, editor Jerome Bennett spoke for thousands of admirers when he referred to Howard Thurman as a "Twentieth Century Holy Man." Indeed, many people sensed a special spiritual quality in this quiet, gifted individual. He was in touch with both God and himself.

Our focus will be upon Howard Thurman's life and work as a modern-day psalmist. We call him this not because of his twenty-three books, many of which are devotional and meditative. Nor do we honor him in this regard because of his work as a poet; rather, we celebrate Howard Thurman as a modern-day psalmist because he shared the heart and soul of the ancient poets of Israel. Thurman often advised his listeners and readers to find a spiritual "clothesline" on which to hang their hopes, and hurts, and dreams.[11] Like the psalmists of old, he looked for spiritual starting points that might quicken his reflections and prayers. His favorite spiritual clothesline was Psalm 139, especially its opening line, "O Lord, thou hast searched me, and known me." These beautiful lines from the King James Version readied Thurman for his exploration of God and a life lived in service of God.

From his earliest days, Thurman sensed that life had an essential unity. But as an African American reared in Daytona, Florida, at the beginning of the twentieth century, he knew that such common ground was very hard to find. He longed to break free from America's racism, which so often denied him the opportunity to search out the deeper meanings of God and community. Indeed, the tentacles of racism reached into every aspect of young Thurman's life, creating a terrible crisis for his sensitive spirit. Racial policies in Daytona schools, for example, prevented blacks from receiving a public high school education. African Americans were graduated from the seventh grade and then denied access to the eighth grade. This kept blacks from acquiring an eighth-grade diploma, which was necessary for entrance into high school.

Fortunately, Thurman was able to circumvent this racist obstacle to a high school education. His elementary school principal tutored him during the summer months after seventh grade until he was prepared to challenge the eighth-grade examination. He did so successfully and received his eighth-grade diploma. However, the possibility of a high school education remained remote. There were only three public high schools for blacks in Florida, and none was near his home in Daytona Beach.[12]

But Howard Thurman would not be denied in his struggle to gain a secondary education. He was enrolled in a private, church-related black high school in Jacksonville. His family worked hard to pay the tuition. Thurman in turn studied and worked hard for his education. Almost at the point of physical exhaustion, he graduated first in his high school class and received a scholarship to Morehouse College. Again, he graduated as valedictorian of his class, having read every book in the college library. He then attended Rochester Divinity School as one of two black students in his class slotted for admission, and once again he graduated first in his class. He had overcome all educational roadblocks, but not without much pain and struggle.

Other racial obstacles were equally difficult to surmount. The daily indignities that black children faced in the racist climate of the South

constantly reminded Thurman that he was a nonperson in the domi-
nant white world. Later, he recalled the effects of such psychological
brutalization:

> I was a very sensitive child who suffered much from the violence of
> racial conflict. The climate of our town, Daytona Beach, Florida, was
> better than most southern towns because of the influence of the
> tourists who wintered there. Nevertheless, life became more and
> more suffocating because of the fear of being brutalized, beaten, or
> otherwise outraged.[13]

Young Thurman experienced frequent assaults upon his dignity as a
human being. Thurman remembers on one occasion that he was
attacked by a five-year-old white girl. While he was raking leaves for her
family, he had become frustrated with this little daughter of his
employer. She kept scattering Thurman's leaf piles as fast as he could
rake them. He lost his temper and scolded her. In anger, the little girl
drew a straight pin out from her dress and stabbed Thurman in his
hand. He reeled back in pain and asked the little girl if she had gone
crazy. Then came the devastating reply, "Oh, Howard, that didn't hurt
you! You can't feel!"[14]

The racist assumption of the white child was clear. Howard Thurman
was a "Negro," and everyone knew that blacks could not feel pain
because they were less than human—this was the obvious racist point.
In this kind of social and cultural climate, it was difficult, if not impossible, for Howard Thurman to find the common ground with God and
others which he sought. And yet he knew at a deeper level that it must
exist. Call it a mystical intuition. But God had already spoken to Thurman of this unity.

Child of God

The larger world as defined by whites lacked common ground. Thus,
Howard Thurman turned to other resources in his spiritual quest.
Gradually, he discovered these in his family, in the world of nature, and
in his black church. First and foremost, his family provided an emotional anchor for him in a turbulent world. This was especially true in
the case of his grandmother, Nancy Ambrose. Born a slave, Nancy
Ambrose had a keen sense of what really mattered in life. We are so
fortunate when God provides that special person who seems to make
all the difference. We have seen how this was true for Augustine and
his friendship with Bishop Ambrose. So it was for Thurman and his
Grandma Nancy.

It was Nancy Ambrose's mission in life to guard and nurture her grandson's sensitive spirit. According to Thurman, whenever his spirit was low, his grandmother would buoy him up with a story from her slave days on a north Florida plantation. In her favorite story, she would recount for her grandson how once a year a slave preacher, that is, a fellow slave, was permitted to preach without the white master being present. This was a redemptive event—a miraculous occasion.

The slave preacher would deliver a powerful biblical sermon that always ended in the same way. Without flinching, he would look his congregation of fellow slaves square in the eye and declare with all the force he could muster, "You are not niggers! You are not slaves. You are God's children."[15] Armed with this theological conviction, Thurman reports that he could face anything the world threw his way. It was a lesson he never forgot. It was a defining moment that filled his spirit. As a child of God, Thurman realized that others had no right to impose their definitions on him. He could not be defined by others. No person, or no group of people, could alter his identity as one who belonged to God. As the psalmist would say, he was known by God. Being a child of God meant for Thurman that he was freed of all racist definitions of his being. He was somebody because, like all of God's creation, he was of God, and no individual or group could define him as a nonperson.

Throughout his adult years, Thurman carried this lesson with him. He also instilled it in others. He helped thousands to realize that they too were children of God, and by such identity they were of infinite worth and dignity. A future generation of civil rights leaders learned this valuable lesson from Thurman, including Martin Luther King Jr. and Jesse Jackson. Dr. Benjamin May, noted educator and former president of Morehouse College, once said that whenever Howard Thurman spoke at colleges and churches people knew they were listening to a free man. Being a child of God, Thurman refused all chains imposed upon him by others. In May's words:

> Those of us who have read his books knew that Howard was a free man. Freedom leaped out in every direction, whether in sermons, articles, books, one knew that Howard was free. He walked like a free man. He wrote like a free man. He spoke like a free man.[16]

The God of freedom was also discovered by Thurman in the world of nature. Much like the ancient psalmist, he was attuned to the many faces of the natural world. Its vast images captured his imagination. Thurman tells us that he was befriended by the woods near his home. The ocean was another of his joyful companions. Like the psalmist, he was led to "lie down in green pastures," and he found himself "beside still waters" (Psalm 23:2–3). He had his own secret hiding place, the oak tree in his backyard. This tree became Thurman's most trusted boyhood friend. Of this friend, he said, "I needed the strength of that tree, and, like it, I wanted to hold my ground. . . . I could reach down in the quiet places of my spirit, take out my bruises and my joys, unfold them and talk about them."[17]

As in the psalms, Thurman could declare of God, "you are a hiding place for me" (Psalm 32:7). In communion with the oak tree, Thurman knew that he was understood. For Thurman, nature pointed beyond itself to its creator, God. The woods, the ocean, and the oak tree evoked a profound awareness of God. There was an undefinable divine-human encounter here, one that many of us may have also experienced. Like Thurman, we may not have precise words for the powerful connection we feel between our spirits and the Something which is in, but not limited to, the natural order. Thurman wrote of his nature experiences, "There were times when it seemed as if the earth and the river and the sky and I were one beat of the same pulse." He added, "There would come a moment when beyond the single pulse beat there was a sense of Presence which seemed always to speak to me." In this Presence, Thurman encountered the Source that he knew to be the center of all life. It was the dynamic power in which we live, and move, and have our being. He has said of these luminous moments: "There was no voice. There was no image. There was no vision. There was God."[18]

Thurman never reduced God to nature, but he did value nature's openings to God. In our *lectio divina* of both the psalms and Thurman, this insight can be a guiding light. God is to be found in wonderful and splendid ways in the world of nature. The natural world remains a marvelous resource for our encounters with God. We should never cut ourselves off from the Creator's natural order of things. If we do so, we may miss many wonderful opportunities to meet God.

Deep River

In addition to family and the natural world, Howard Thurman's most profound spiritual experiences came from within the black church. And at the heart of this encounter was the Negro spiritual. As Walter Fluker and Catherine Tumber suggest in *A Strange Freedom,* "these songs were staples of worship and spiritual expression" for Howard Thurman.[19] In fact, Thurman would refer to these songs often when he sought to discern the meaning of his relationship with God.

Thurman's own work, *Deep River,* provides us with an excellent example of how the spirituals enriched his understanding of God and the human condition. The particular human experience expressed in the spirituals was that of the African American slave. Thurman said that the Negro spiritual provided "a windbreak" for his "forefathers against the brutalities of slavery." He said they established "a ground of hope undimmed by the contradictions which held them in tight embrace."[20] This hope, argued Thurman, presented a deep spiritual grounding not only for the slave but also for the work of protest and liberation that subsequent generations of African Americans embraced.

Like the psalms, the spirituals of African Americans are not limited to their time and place. In addition to the soulful encouragement they have given generations of African Americans, they also teach all humanity about life and death, suffering and triumph. Whether we are black or white, male or female, free or slave, the spirituals speak to that which is deepest in the human experience.

In *Deep River*, Thurman explored the universal dimensions of the spirituals. He used the image of the river, found in several of these songs, as a metaphor for life—a life ultimately touched by God's loving current. He often quoted from the spiritual called "Deep River," which he had sung in the black church of his youth:

> Deep River, my home is over Jordan;
> Deep River, my home is over Jordan.
> O don't you want to go to that Gospel Feast
> That Promised Land where all is Peace?
> Deep River, I want to cross over into camp ground.[21]

For Thurman, this song of faith expressed both the particular and most universal longings of the slave. As he notes, "To slip over the river from one of the border states would mean a chance for freedom in the North—or, to cross the river into Canada would mean freedom in a new country, a foreign land."[22] But the song also contained a broader meaning.

According to Thurman, the river in the song exists as "a full and creative analogy" for life itself and its movement toward God. In the first place, he reasoned, rivers have simple beginnings. Yet it is the nature of a river to flow from its source. Thurman says, "Life is like that."[23] We move from our almost imperceptible origins into the great currents of life. Like a river we too are always on our way, always living in a dynamic and changing flow toward the sea—our goal.

Also the river is alive! Thurman writes, "It's this aliveness that generates and sustains all the particular manifestations of life." All judgments about our lives, and other lives, are by nature incomplete because our lives, like the river, never stand still. "It is for this reason that in the last analysis judgment belongs with God," reasons Thurman.[24] He expands on his analogy. We are perhaps most like the banks of the river.

> Every bank that is touched by a river gives of itself to the water. It has no option: it is the nature of the relationship that the bank yield of itself to the river that drains it. . . . Life is like that! If we think for a moment of the individual as the bank of the river and of life as the river, the analogy becomes fascinating.[25]

Thus, for Thurman, we are in relationship with all of life, whether we choose to be or not. Our lives, like the banks of a river, are constantly being shaped by the river—by life itself. In times of drought, our lives dry up and become parched, and the crack lines, like those of the river banks, become visible. During flood times, our lives may roll on with a mighty force, like water over a river bank—we might even be over-whelmed and carried along on a tide of events beyond our control. And God, "the Paradox of paradoxes," is at the center of it all.[26]

We are in relation to God just as the river is in relation to its source and goal—the sea. "From gurgling spring to giant waterfall; from morning dew to torrential downpour; from simple creeks to mighty river," writes Thurman, "the source and the goal are the same: the sea." In like manner, he muses, "That out of which life comes is that into which life goes."[27] This is the nature of the living God for Thurman. Perhaps this is why Thurman sometimes refers to God as the "Bot-tomer" of existence. There is nothing of greater depth—everything, ourselves included, begins and ends with God.

Thurman's metaphor of the river concludes with his conviction that life loses its meaning if it is cut off from its source and goal—God. Without a connection to our source and goal, we are without clear def-inition. We are literally without shape or form—a river without banks or water, without a wellspring or a sea.

The psalmist and Howard Thurman agree. We are a deep river. God's movement into and out of us is relentless. We can be thrown off course temporarily as the river flows to the sea. But flow it must. Thur-man says of those of us who wander, "they [we] may wander for a mil-lion years in desert and waste land, through sin and degradation, war and pestilence, hate and love—at last they [we] must find their [our] rest in Him."[28] It cannot be otherwise. Of this the psalmist and Thur-man are certain. All rivers eventually lead to the sea.

PART TWO

Living with Hope

CHAPTER FIVE

The Rainbow People of God

God said, "This is the sign of the covenant that I make between me and you and every living creature that is with you, for all future generations: I have set my bow in the clouds, and it shall be a sign of the covenant between me and the earth. . . . When the bow is in the clouds, I will see it and remember the everlasting covenant between God and every living creature of all flesh that is on the earth."

GENESIS 9:12–13, 16

At home in South Africa I have sometimes said in big meetings where you have black and white together: "Raise your hands!" Then I've said, "Move your hands—different colors representing different people. You are the rainbow people of God." And you remember the rainbow in the Bible is the sign of peace. The rainbow is the sign of prosperity. We want peace, prosperity and justice and we can have it when all the people of God, the rainbow people of God work together.

DESMOND TUTU, PREACHING IN NORWAY (1991)

WE ALL LIVE UNDER THE SAME SKY. We all inhabit the same earth, and according to Genesis and Archbishop Desmond Tutu of South Africa, we all are created by the same God. For century upon century God's rainbow has served as the symbol of that unity. Indeed, the rainbow symbolizes the Creator's intent that we all might be one in peace and prosperity. The rainbow exists as a constant reminder of this divine hope and promise.

But many people are yet to catch the vision of this rainbow reality. As was true in Noah's generation, we are far too willing to accept the idea that separateness and division are the natural order of things. The priestly writers of Genesis, and Desmond Tutu, have said no to this greatest of human deceptions. There is a far better way, they claim, marked by the sign of the rainbow. It promises a different kind of future. This future differs from our projections forward from the present. This rainbow hope is the inbreaking of God's future. It is the point of departure for this chapter's *lectio divina*.

According to the story of the rainbow, we live as a people of hope. Jesus, schooled in the ancient story of the rainbow, understood this most basic of truths. It was encoded deep within his spiritual genes. In fact, Jesus embodied God's hope for humanity through his own glorious rainbow resurrection. As we shall discover, rainbow and resurrection mean the same thing in God's reckoning—new life! In his earthly ministry, Jesus was turning us back to the ancient and eternal truth of the rainbow promise. God is not done with us yet! As Desmond Tutu has reminded us, we are called forth to be the rainbow people of God. Our hope, especially our hope in Christ, depends upon our response to this great truth of God symbolized first by the rainbow and then again by the resurrection.

Real Sin

The priestly writers of the Old Testament knew of difficult times. Writing about five hundred years before Jesus, they had lived through the destruction of their nation at the hands of the Babylonians. Jerusalem had been conquered and the temple of God destroyed. Carried off into captivity, those of Judah who survived sat down by the waters of Babylon and wept (Psalm 137). They lamented their separation from God. They had failed to keep the covenant; they had been idolatrous in their worship; and they had not promoted peace and justice throughout the land.

In brief, the priestly writers, along with the prophets, confessed that Judah and all of Israel had alienated themselves from God. They were now suffering the consequences of their own sinfulness. They had turned their back on God and God's teachings, the Torah. In this state of severe crisis, they slowly began to remember. Reaching back into history, before the glory days of David and Moses, the priestly writers remembered an even better time—the time of beginnings, the time of creation itself.

The priestly writers looked back to when the world was young and everything in it was fresh and new. After their people's exile and return to Jerusalem, they began to recall ancient stories revealed by God about the origins of the earth and the heavens and human life itself. As sacred scribes, they wrote these stories and edited them with a renewed enthusiasm for the holy acts of creation. They reminded a broken and recovering nation how God had created a marvelous world originally filled with promise and hope.

In the first chapter of Genesis, the priestly writers record how God set the world in motion through the spoken word. The waters and dry lands were parted, and the earth was populated by plants and animals of all shapes and sizes until human beings themselves emerged as the crowning act of the Creator. Everything was now set in motion. And we humans were said to be created in the very image of God:

> So God created humankind in his image,
>   in the image of God he created them;
>   male and female he created them.
> GENESIS 1:27

But something went horribly wrong. Sin entered the world. According to the priestly writers, God took a real chance with humanity. The Creator granted us the gift of freedom—the very stuff of God. But we used this great gift against the Creator's intent. Instead of taking our place within the harmony of God's creation, we chose instead to lord it over God's creation and one another. Rather than respecting God and God's creation, we wanted to replace God with ourselves, in fact to be God—the original sin. In the greatest power play in history, we used God's gift of freedom, our free will, against God for our own gratification and selfish ends. This led to destructive consequences of which the priestly writers were painfully aware. Very quickly disaster set in.

A series of events are recorded in Genesis that caused the Creator to have second thoughts about creation. Almost like a potter, God wondered whether it might not be time to recast the clay and form a new vessel. Adam and Eve had disobeyed God and eaten the forbidden fruit. Expelled from their paradise garden, the first murder is committed as their son Cain slew his younger brother Abel. Then, after only ten generations, the whole world is filled with violence, and we are told that Noah's generation knew no peace.

The Flood and the Rainbow

By the time of the story of the flood in Genesis 6, there are few good people left on earth. Almost everyone has been consumed by greed and violence. Noah, however, was a shining exception. In Genesis 6:9 we read,

"Noah was a righteous man, blameless in his generation." He was said to have "walked with God." Others, unlike Noah, chose in their God-given freedom to not walk with God but to chart their own selfish courses.

In Genesis 5, Noah appears to us almost as a second Adam, a second father of the human race. He is the first gardener and keeper of the vines. Biblical scholar Terence Fretheim has suggested, "After the murder perpetuated by Cain and the vengeful response of Lamech, Genesis 5 may represent a fresh start. . . ."[1] But too much damage already appears to have been done. God cannot find enough reason for the world's preservation in its present, violent stage, and so he destroys it. This is a harsh ending to a world turned in upon itself. The Creator decides to start over. But Noah is a righteous man, and so he and his family are spared along with an ark full of animals (Genesis 6–9). The very length of the Noah story, with its flood account, attests to the importance placed upon this event by the priestly writers. It is the longest, and I would argue, the most important of the early Genesis stories. And I say this because of its theology.

Within the story of Noah and the flood, and the story of the sign of the rainbow, we can find a fascinating and ultimately compassionate picture of God. It has taken me many years to see this, for at first gloss all that is seen is a destructive God who nearly obliterates creation and everything in it. I can remember as a child looking at artists' renderings of the great flood with doomed men, women, and children frantically clinging to rocks as the waters rise to drown them unmercifully.

The flood story does contain disaster and judgment. According to the Bible, the wickedness (mainly greed and violence) of humans was indeed great. Because of this, God repents of his creation and determines to destroy the world (Genesis 6:5–13). Only the righteous Noah and his family are to be spared (Genesis 6:8–9). God announces his intentions and orders Noah to build an ark (Genesis 6:13–17; 7:4). Members of every species of animal, along with Noah's family, are boarded on the ark, and they ride out the storm and rains for forty days and forty nights. After a further passage of time, the waters recede and all the inhabitants of the ark step out onto dry land, once again to repopulate the earth (Genesis 6–8).

Finally, the rainbow is set "in the clouds" as a sign of the covenant between God and all future inhabitants of the earth, including "every living creature of all flesh" (Genesis 9:12–15). It is to remind God that this kind of destruction shall not occur again. God declares, "When the bow is in the clouds, I will see it and remember the everlasting covenant between God and every living creature of all flesh that is on the earth"

(Genesis 9:16). In order to reinforce God's renewed commitment to humanity, the next and closing verse declares: "God said to Noah, 'This is the sign of the covenant that I have established between me and all flesh that is on the earth' " (Genesis 9:17).

All about God

The story of Noah, the flood, and the rainbow is about God more than it is about humanity. The most basic question concerns what the Creator is to do with a creation so marred and corrupted by self-interest, greed, and violence. Looking carefully at Genesis 6–9, we discover that God "appears, not as an angry and vengeful judge, but as a grieving and pained parent."[2] Distraught at our misuse of freedom for selfish ends, the text says that "the Lord was sorry that he had made humankind on the earth, and it grieved him to his heart" (Genesis 6:6). According to Fretheim, "grieved" may even be too weak a translation for the Hebrew term *nikami*.[3] It is more like unlimited pain, the excruciating pain God felt when the self-centered and violent actions of humanity destroyed creation's original balance and harmony. This pain must have been almost unbearable for God.

God, whose heart has been broken, then announces judgment. But being the good Parent, the Creator also looks for some way to redeem the situation. And so God finds a glimmer of hope in Noah, the righteous man. As Fretheim observes, "God's gracious choice of Noah results from the divine agony over what to do about the creation."[4]

It is God who takes the initiative and seeks to salvage something from the world's self-centered demise. Notice the Lord personally shuts the door on the ark, and when the waters subside, God once again personally orders everyone out of the ark. The priestly writers wanted to make it clear that God remains interested in the world's future. The Creator refuses to be resigned to the presence of sin. God will instead teach humanity through prophets and sages about a far better way. In the new rainbow reality God decides to value and care for creation unconditionally, regardless of human shortcomings. The postflood world will never be without a sign of God's sustaining love. This will be true all the way to the foot of the cross.

In order to affirm these decisions, God establishes a universal covenant with humanity and all living things. This will be the first of many covenants, or agreements, set forth by God in the Bible. And it is a special one. Here the relationship established by the Creator is not only with Israel, as important as that is, but also with all peoples of the earth. The rainbow becomes the eternal symbol of this loving and hope-filled arrangement. The rainbow comes after the storm; the bow of prismatic colors is formed against the background of the passing clouds. First the troubled skies, then the clearing of the heavens for God's loving rainbow. If God is for us, who can be against us? (Romans 8:31).

This is the true hope of God's rainbow reality. Out of love the Creator exercises self-limits on divine power so that in freedom we might continue to grow up into the image of God. We are free to bring judgment upon ourselves, but we are also free to love one another under God's rainbow reality. The Lord holds forth this hope, and there are always some who understand and embrace all the colors of this grace-filled rainbow. Desmond Tutu is one such man.

Desmond Tutu, the Rainbow Man

Nowhere are rainbows more beautiful than in sub-Saharan Africa. At Victoria Falls in Zimbabwe, I have stood in silence and amazement before the roaring mist and multiple rainbows produced by the cascading Zambezi River. But not even this grandeur matches the grace and dignity of the rainbow man of Africa, Desmond Tutu. I met the then Archbishop of Cape Town in January 1996, and for me it was a thrill of a lifetime. What Tutu had accomplished in the name of Christ and nonviolence in South Africa has resulted in millions of admirers from around the world.

We stood face to face in an academic courtyard on the beautiful hillside campus of the University of Cape Town. "Thank you," I said, "for all you have done [to end apartheid]." As we shook hands and introduced ourselves, I was struck by the way in which this physically small individual managed to fill the entire courtyard with his presence. I wondered how this could be. Then I realized that this is the rainbow man of God. His very presence radiates peace.

Nelson Mandela has praised Desmond Tutu as the embodiment of hope for all oppressed peoples of South Africa. He has stood as a beacon of light for those who have lived through the evils of apartheid, the government-mandated separation of races. In fact, Tutu's courageous leadership against apartheid in the name of Christ became legendary throughout the world and in 1991 he was awarded the Nobel Peace Prize. Beginning late in 1995, he chaired the Truth and Reconciliation Commission of post-apartheid South Africa, bringing healing to a deeply wounded nation. However, this diminutive witness for peace and justice has known as many storms as he has rainbows. His journey to peace has been a tumultuous struggle for freedom. But as we shall see, it has never been a struggle without hope, not even in the bleakest of times.

Born in 1931 in Klerksdorp, a gold-mining town west of Johannesburg, Tutu was seventeen when the white South African electorate

voted the National Party into power, and with it the mandate to introduce apartheid. This meant that he and millions of other South
Africans of color were to have no vote and no say in their country's
future. By 1950 the Population Registration Act had enforced a classi-
fication of all individuals by race: white, African (black), Indian, and
colored (mixed race). Under apartheid only the powerful white minority had open access to government, quality education, and economic
prosperity.

Tutu and his family, classified as African, were disfranchised and
denied the most basic of freedoms, including the ability to make decisions regarding their own future. Hope for a better tomorrow was cut
off and denied. Tutu's father was a successful educator in missionary
schools. His mother was a domestic servant, a gentle woman known
popularly as Komotso because of her care for the afflicted. But living
under the laws of apartheid was a humiliating experience for the Tutu
family. Much later Tutu was to write:

> You are brainwashed into an acquiescence in your oppression and
> exploitation. You come to believe what others have determined about
> you, filling you with self-disgust, self-contempt and self-hatred,
> accepting a negative image . . . and you need a lot of grace to have
> that demon of self-hatred exorcised, when you accept that only white
> races really matter and you allow the white person to set your stan-
> dards and provide your role models.[5]

With all these limitations, Tutu prepared himself as an educator to
follow in his father's footsteps. Until 1953 most African education was
in the hands of church schools, and here Tutu thought he could teach
with some measure of dignity. However, the Bantu Education Act
changed this and established control by the central government over all
African schools. This takeover of the educational system by the
apartheid government led Tutu to abandon his first career out of
protest. He could not participate in the oppression of his own people.

Where was Tutu to turn? What was next for him in his native land?
His anguished and monumental decision to leave education—for he
was an excellent teacher—was followed by a life-changing decision to
train for the priesthood. On his own admission, his motives to become
a priest were a combination of idealism and practicality. Tutu had been
a deeply committed Christian, actively involved in the Anglican church.
But he also needed a job. And so he entered theological college freely
admitting that his reasons were not completely noble.[6]

Desmond Tutu grew into the priesthood in ways that may have surprised him, but not God. By the end of 1961, at thirty years of age,
Tutu had become an ordained priest. During this time, political unrest

filled the country. But Tutu as a new priest in Johannesburg had remained essentially inactive in the growing political protests against apartheid, although he had strong personal feelings about its injustices. All this, however, was soon to change as God gently moved this fledgling priest into the public arena of the struggle against apartheid.

Destruction and Dignity

By the mid-1960s, it had become clear to Desmond Tutu that South Africa was destroying itself. A land whose people and natural beauty he loved was consuming itself because of the destructive effects of its national government's policies of apartheid. To use an analogy from Genesis, the waters of hatred and division were on the rise, and the whole of the land was about to be swallowed up by its own injustices and violence.

In 1960, after the Sharpeville massacre of young Africans by government forces, the protesting African National Congress (ANC) and Pan African Congress (PAC) were banned by the government as seditious. This meant the silencing of apartheid's major opponents within South Africa. Soon Nelson Mandela and other anti-apartheid leaders were jailed, and by 1967 the ANC had begun its guerrilla warfare against a rigid and inflexible South African government. One by one African, Indian, colored, and even white voices of opposition were silenced. Who then was to speak?

The hand of God fell upon Desmond Tutu. He was to become the voice for those who had no voice. In *Tutu: Voice of the Voiceless,* Shirley Du Boulay has characterized Tutu's response to God's prodding in the words of Shakespeare: "Some are born great, some achieve greatness, some have greatness thrust upon them." She claims, "Desmond's achievements belong to the third of these categories, though greatness was not so much thrust upon him as emerging, with a remorseless inevitability, from his religious beliefs."[7] Tutu would quickly become God's rainbow man, a living sign of hope for the oppressed peoples of South Africa. He began to live as a free man even as his government denied him his most basic human rights.

Tutu had long believed that a priest's first duty was to bring a sense of worth and dignity to his parishioners. And apartheid could not alter this. As a Christian leader he told priests under his charge:

> You can sit all day in your house and not visit your people, not take communion to the sick, to the aged, and nobody will usually complain to you, but your church will grow emptier. You can't love people and not visit them. You can't love them unless you know them, and you can't know them unless you visit them regularly. A good shepherd knows his sheep by name.[8]

Likewise, the oppressed of South Africa could not be ignored and abandoned. By the 1970s most of the political opposition to apartheid had been imprisoned, exiled, or murdered by the South African government. Who then was left to speak out, if not the church? It fell to brave men and women like Bishop Desmond Tutu of Johannesburg to care not only for the souls in his church but also the soul of his nation. The God-given dignity of every South African—oppressed and oppressors—must be restored. This was the rainbow challenge.

The Rainbow People of God

On September 13, 1989, the impossible happened. In a spectacle not seen before in South Africa, an enormous crowd of some thirty thousand people moved freely through the streets of Cape Town in protest against apartheid. Archbishop Desmond Tutu, the first black African to head the Anglican church in the southern region of Africa, was at the front of the protest march as it made its way to city hall. Linking arms in solidarity with black, Indian, colored, and white South Africans who said no to apartheid, Tutu made the following remarks:

> I'm just an old man after all these fiery speeches. . . . But I want to say to you: today is the day in which we the people have scored a great victory for justice and for peace. And it is important that it is registered. . . . We can say, "There is nothing wrong with South Africa except for the perpetrators of apartheid." No, no, no. We believe they can change. So let us not say, "except for the perpetrators of apartheid."
>
> There is nothing wrong with this beautiful country except for apartheid! There is nothing wrong with this beautiful country except for injustice! There is nothing wrong with this country except for the violence of apartheid! . . .
>
> This country is a rainbow country! This country is Technicolor. You can come and see the new South Africa![9]

Beginning with his 1976 letter to the prime minister warning of violence in South Africa, Desmond Tutu had worked tirelessly for a nonviolent overthrow of apartheid. He had become public enemy number one for the apartheid government of the late 1970s and 1980s. In his position as general secretary of the South African Council of Churches, Tutu had been relentless in his opposition to apartheid's evils. Harassed, arrested, and discredited by the government-controlled media, Tutu nonetheless persevered. Even threats against his life and the life of family members did not deter him.

Tutu was convinced on theological grounds, not because of political ideology, that apartheid was wrong. Not long before the Cape Town march, Tutu had written a public response to Prime Minister P. W. Botha, who had made public a private letter from Tutu. Tutu declared that his government's policies related to apartheid were "unbiblical, unchristian, immoral and evil."[10] Accused of being a Marxist and a mouthpiece of the banned ANC, Tutu made clear that his position on apartheid was derived from the Bible—from an ancient faith that had predated communism and modern African politics by many, many centuries.

Tutu reiterated in this letter what he had said so many times before: "The Bible teaches that what invests each person with infinite value is not this or that arbitrarily chosen biological attribute, but the fact that each person is created in the image of God (Genesis 1:26)."[11] Furthermore, he told Botha, "I could show that apartheid teaches the fundamental irreconcilability of people because they belong to different races." Tutu stated flatly, "This is at variance with the central teaching of the Christian faith about the reconciling work of our Lord and Saviour Jesus Christ . . . (2 Corinthians 5:9; . . . John 12:32; Ephesians 1:10; Ephesians 2:14 etc.)."[12]

Tutu further insisted, "I have not deviated from the teachings of our church on this matter at any point."[13] He refused to permit his detractors to misrepresent his position. When accused of being an agent of the ANC who used his religious position for purely political ends, the archbishop firmly recalled his recent face-to-face meeting with Botha: "I told you in my interview that I support the ANC in its objectives to establish a nonracial, democratic South Africa; but I do not support its methods."[14] As a Christian religious leader, Tutu stated, "I am committed to work for a nonracial, just and democratic South Africa."[15] Not to do so would be to deny the gospel itself. Apartheid was not primarily a political issue for Tutu; it was a matter of faith or faithlessness.

During the Cape Town march, Desmond Tutu made a second speech in which he made his commitment to God's kingdom of justice and peace clear. Even the despair of decades of suffering and disappointment was no match for the power of the anti-apartheid movement. The waters of hatred and violence, in this historic moment, had begun to recede. Speaking outside the city hall of Cape Town's Grand Parade, Tutu repeated the main points of his previous remarks inside city hall. This was followed by great cheers from the massive crowd. Then the archbishop called for silence. In a short, dramatic statement referring to the purple dye used in the water cannons for crowd control by security forces of the government, Tutu declared:

Let's just keep quiet. "Mr. de Klerk, did you hear a pin drop?" They tried to make us one color: purple. We say we are the rainbow people! We are the new people of the new South Africa![16]

Desmond Tutu knew in his heart that evil never has the last word. Even in the darkest of times, he knew of the rainbow promise of God. He knew we can live as a people of hope because God has pledged not to abandon us.

Nearly five years after the Cape Town march, Tutu once again stood at the same city hall balcony before Cape Town's Grand Parade, but this time to introduce a new state president, Nelson Mandela. As he did, he stated once again the unofficial credo of the new South Africa, a credo that he in faith had affirmed so many times before. "We of many cultures, languages and races are become one nation. We are the Rainbow People of God."[17]

South Africa has progressed toward its vision of a nonracial, democratic society, but it has not reached the end of its arduous journey. We too have far to go. But the rainbow still appears after the storm, and our hearts are stirred once again to the hope of God's promise. Thanks be to God for rainbows and resurrections.

CHAPTER SIX

All Will Be Well

For I am convinced that neither death, nor life,
nor angels, nor rulers, nor things present, nor
things to come, nor powers, nor height, nor depth,
nor anything in all creation, will be able to separate
us from the love of God in Christ Jesus our Lord.

ROMANS 8:38

I felt the pain, and afterwards the joy and the
delight, now the one and now the other, again
and again, I suppose about twenty times. And in
the time of joy I could have said with Paul: nothing shall separate me from the love of Christ; and
in the pain, I could have said with Peter: Lord,
save me, I am perishing.

JULIAN OF NORWICH, *Showings*

THE APOSTLE PAUL'S CONFIDENCE in God seems unshakable. Nothing,
he claims in his letter to Christians at Rome, "will be able to separate
us from the love of God in Christ Jesus." And lest we forget, this affirmation of faith is that of a man who five different times received thirty-
nine lashes for preaching the gospel. He was also shipwrecked three
times during his missionary journeys, faced bandits on the roads, and
experienced great hostility from Jews and Gentiles in many Mediterranean cities.

Everywhere Paul turned, he seemed threatened with injury or death
because of his faith (2 Corinthians 11: 23–29). But he persisted in his
commitment to proclaim the hope of God's gospel of love and reconciliation in Christ. We find a similar hope expressed in the witness of a
medieval Christian called Julian of Norwich. Living during the fourteenth century, a time filled with plagues, religious wars, and church

corruption, she managed to express a tremendous hope that "all will be well" because of God's persistent love. Julian's faith, like Paul's, came out of dire circumstances.

In her youth, Julian nearly died of an unknown disease. She then lived out her frail life in voluntary separation from the world as an anchoress, a person secluded in a life of prayer and meditation. And although she didn't experience the external threats that challenged Paul, the internal journey of her soul was plagued by spiritual burdens similar to those that confronted the apostle during much of his public ministry. Whether the enemy is external or internal (and it usually is both), the struggle to keep hope alive is always a challenge.

Beginning with Paul's letter to the Romans, we want to ask in this chapter what gives Paul and Julian the courage of their convictions. Looking at Paul's letter to the Romans and Julian's writings in *Showings*, we want to discover the basis for their confident living. What role does hope play in the lives of Paul and Julian? And more to the point, how can Paul and Julian, our silent partners in conversation, help us to realize the possibility of God's in-breaking hope for our own lives?

Faith's Mountaintop

In my reading of the New Testament, the greatest peak of faith is to be found in the eighth chapter of Romans. Here, Paul scales to a spiritual height that few, if any, have equaled in the annals of devotional writing. At the close of Romans 8, he summarizes the joyous outcome of living a life in Christ; namely, the love of God that will never leave us. In very few words, Paul unlocks faith's meaning for us: What confirms our faith is not who we are, but who God is. God is the one who loves us and never gives up on us.

The remarkable thing about Paul's affirmation of faith and hope for the future is that it is born out of personal suffering, distress, and failure. If anyone had a right to give up on God, it was Paul. And yet he insisted, God's love in Christ Jesus prevails. In unabashed faith, Paul declares from his own experience that nothing can displace God's love for us. Neither life or death nor rulers or things past or present can separate us from the love of God in Christ Jesus.

The apostle believed that whatever our past, we are not prisoners to it. This is a word that we need to hear almost every day. It seems the longer we live, the more we have to regret. Often, we can't get beyond those things that have bound us. But Paul's word to us is we don't have to be enslaved to our past—or for that matter, the present. Nothing in all creation can finally keep us from the love of Christ. Romans 8 presents us with the apostle's most succinct affirmation of this kind of hope-filled faith—a new life in Christ. We are to live outside the box of our past and present. Since we know our future is secure in God, we need not be afraid.

But the question comes back to us: how do we reach such heights of faith? Intellectually we acknowledge that faith is not of our own making. It is in itself a gift from God. But our hearts still need to be transformed. Indeed, this is what our silent conversations with Scripture are all about. Hearing the Word of God, how do we respond with both head and heart? Paul, in all his complexity, has been a faithful and hopeful guide for me in these matters.

To be sure, Paul's teachings on sin, grace, justification, and reconciliation have deeply influenced Christianity. But as with Jesus himself, when I look at Paul it is the life that means the most to me. This particular insight into Paul and his faith has occurred to me during two distinct readings of Romans 8. I mention these two accounts to remind us that living encounters with the Bible prevent us from fixed meanings and singular interpretations. After all, God continues to speak to us through the Scriptures, and our understanding of God's Word continues to grow and deepen.

The first time I read Romans 8 was as a teenager. I was to preach my first sermon in front of my hometown church (at the ripe old age of eighteen) and I had decided upon Romans 8 as my text. I don't remember if it was instinct or whether someone had told me, but I knew there was something important at the end of the eighth chapter of Romans. I knew very little about this letter. Later I learned that Romans was the most carefully constructed of Paul's letters within the New Testament. Unlike his other letters, this one wasn't written in the heat of controversy. Rather, it was written in a reflective mood to Christians far away in Rome. Since Paul had not as yet met most of these brothers and sisters in the faith, his letter served as an introduction of himself, and even more important, of the gospel message he proclaimed.

Even in my youth, I was aware of the mountaintop of faith that Paul takes the reader to in the eighth chapter. Who could miss it? Everything in the chapter, indeed in the letter itself, led me to one essential point: Nothing in all creation can separate us from the love of God in Christ Jesus. It was, and is, for me a Christ-like mantra repeated over and over by Paul in his writings. So I turned to Romans 8 and preached with all my youthful sincerity a sermon entitled "The Victory That Is Ours." The one thing I remember for certain about this sermon is that it was awful. I had borrowed freely from a Peter Marshall sermon and added a few lyrics from a rock-n-roll song. There was nothing memorable about this first sermon except for one thing: those who heard me preach that day raved about the sermon. The congregation was filled with encouragement for a scared but earnest teenager whose potential as a preacher was somewhere far removed in the distant future. But they had hope for me, a foretaste of the hope that is ours in Christ Jesus.

Many years later as I now return to Romans 8 for the writing of this chapter, I'm amazed at how right my choice of texts had been so long ago. If I preached on Romans 8 today, it would not express the easy triumphalism of my youthful faith. Somehow the victories (and for that matter, the defeats) are not as important as they once were. Who knows in God's providence what is a victory and what is a defeat? Even the language of winning someone to Christ doesn't feel quite right anymore. It is not about winning or losing but about being faithful and encouraging faithfulness in others. It is about living in hope!

Paul wanted the Christians at Rome to know that above everything else they were loved by God. This gave hope for the future. This is all I truly wanted to convey to my hometown church—God loves you; after all, isn't that what they had taught me? I was only holding up a mirror and reflecting God's love and hope for us all, both then and now.

Paul's Mirror

Many times Paul is portrayed to us as a complex and sometimes troubled individual. But in the end, all Paul tried to do was hold up the mirror of God's love. Paul was saying to us, Look what glorious thing has happened to me; it can happen to you as well. God's love for you in Christ Jesus can change your life forever. You too can become a new person freed by God to live a life of love. Herein lies the hope. This is the good news that so overpowered Paul. He tried his best to explain his new life in Christ, with varying degrees of success. At times the message got entangled with the cultural values of his time. But at other times he rose above these limitations and got everything right. What a challenge it is for all of us to carry the gospel in our "earthen vessels."

I like A. C. Purdy's description of Paul. This biblical scholar says that Paul "was born into a conflict of cultures."[1] His heritage was strict Judaism (Philippians 3:5–6), but he was also a Jew of the Diaspora, the dispersion of Jews outside of Israel and Judah. Many scholars agree that Paul was from Tarsus in Asia Minor, as is indicated in the book of Acts. In his Mediterranean world, Paul would have experienced a crossroads of cultures; Hellenistic, Roman, and Jewish. We know from his letters that as a Diaspora Jew he wrote in Greek and used a Greek translation of the Old Testament, the Septuagint. But he also knew the language, laws, and customs of his Jewish tradition, having studied, probably in Jerusalem, as a Pharisee.

As a Jew, Paul was at odds with the popular culture of the Mediterranean world. His belief in one God would have set him apart. According to Purdy, "Hardly an ancient writer has a kind word to say about the Jews."[2] Their belief in one God made them square pegs in the round cultural holes of the Greco-Roman world. Their religious devotion to monotheism and their ethical honesty, while admirable, were seldom emulated by others.

Paul also lived in a volatile political world. Even before his conversion to Christianity, he had felt the heavy weight of the Roman imperium upon his people, Israel. Once a Christian, he was in double jeopardy. He was now persecuted by both Jewish and Roman leaders. However, his Roman citizenship (through his family most probably) kept him alive long enough to be tried before a Roman court in Rome itself. There he died, probably under Nero's persecution, still attempting to spread an outlawed gospel.

We are left with the impression that Paul must have been a commanding figure, a hero of faith whose personal appeal must have been as compelling as his spiritual acumen. But this appears not to be so. His letters were indeed powerful and spoke a truth about God in Christ that has endured the test of time. But Paul's letters were probably more effective than either his personal appearance or his preaching. Much to his credit, Paul seemed to recognize this about himself. He knew his strengths and weaknesses, an often overlooked spiritual gift in and of itself. Quoting from words of his opponents in 2 Corinthians 10:10, Paul writes, "They say, 'His letters are weighty and strong, but his bodily presence is weak, and his speech is contemptible.' " An exaggeration perhaps, but not a complete fabrication on the part of his opponents—and Paul knew it! Paul also speaks of a weakness of the flesh (2 Corinthians 12:7–8) that made him less than attractive. Scholars speculate that this might have been epilepsy, malaria, an eye malady (Galatians 6:11), or a physical deformity.

We know enough about Paul to dissuade us of any romantic (heroic) notion that his courageous faith was matched by a charismatic personality. This should serve as a reminder to us that faithfulness is not to be compared with outward appearances. Raymond Brown, one of the twentieth century's greatest biblical scholars, gives us a graphic picture of what true faithfulness entailed for the apostle. He speaks of the daily obstacles Paul faced. He reports, for example, "It is often affirmed that the famous Roman road network facilitated the spread of Christianity, and films about Roman times picture chariots dashing along the roads paved with hard rock."[3] But for Brown, this can be deceiving when thinking about Paul's situation. Paul did take advantage of good Roman roads, but most often he did not have easy access. "Paul," according to Brown, "was an itinerant artisan [tentmaker] who would have had to struggle to get money for food; a wheeled vehicle would have been beyond his means."[4] To fully appreciate Paul's physical hardships, I want to elaborate on Brown's observations:

> Horseback travel was difficult; for horses were not used for long distances, and skill was required in riding (given the absence of the saddles and stirrups that we know). Probably Paul would not even have been able or willing to spend money for a donkey to carry his baggage, for soldiers were prone to requisition these animals from travelers who could not offer resistance. And so we have to picture Paul trudging along the roads, carrying his limited possessions in a sack, at the maximum covering twenty miles a day.[5]

Here, then, was "a Jew with a knapsack on his back" traveling about challenging the Roman Empire with an astounding message that God's love has been revealed through the life, death, and resurrection of a Palestinian Jew. This message, Paul believed, was salvation for the entire world, to Jew and Gentile alike (Galatians 3:28). But who was going to listen? Who would have any faith in Paul's proclamations? Was there to be any real hope in this obscure message?

Brown's characterization of the contempt Paul would have faced from sophisticated Romans and Greeks as a "babbling ragpicker of ideas" is quite accurate. Also, we shouldn't forget the pain of Paul's rejection by his own people both inside and outside of Palestine. Many Jews considered Paul a dangerous, blasphemous proponent of Jesus' messiahship. He was frequently expelled from synagogues as a troublemaker. And according to his letter to the Galatians, he had to prove himself even to his own brothers and sisters within the Christian faith. Many in the Christian churches doubted his claim to discipleship and questioned his motives.

With this kind of rejection, physical hardship, beatings, and imprisonment, how did Paul persevere? Why did he subject himself to this kind of grief? Where was his hope? The answer comes from only one place: his experience of Jesus as the risen Christ. No other answer makes sense. Paul did not put his life on the line for vague ideas or fuzzy principles. He risked all for the living Lord.

Without reservations, Paul committed himself to a person who had changed his life forever, the one he called Christ Jesus. Nothing else had any ultimate significance for the apostle. In a letter to the church at Philippi, he writes: "I regard everything as loss because of the surpassing value of knowing Christ Jesus my Lord" (Philippians 3:8). This brings us to the center of Paul's witness. His faith and hope are in knowing Christ Jesus.

Knowing Christ

Sometimes I am frustrated by friends who say that all you need to do is know Jesus Christ and your life will change in remarkable ways. I don't doubt that this is truth, but I have been put off by how often this profession has been trivialized. Sometimes, I think, it is all made to seem far too easy. Bow your head, raise your hand, be baptized, say the name above all names, praise the Lord! All well and good, but there must be genuine commitment too—something akin to the life-changing discipleship of Paul. We mustn't forget that it was only through his trials and tribulations that Paul came to know the living Christ.

Along these lines, we are sometimes misled by our interpretations of Paul's conversion story. Three times the book of Acts recounts for us the dramatic story of the apostle's experience of the risen Christ on the road to Damascus. While on his way to persecute followers of Christ, Paul the Pharisee (Saul in Hebrew) is knocked from his horse under a blinding light. The details in the accounts vary slightly, but the main point is not lost: "Saul, Saul, why do you persecute me?" Paul asks who speaks these words. The answer is unmistakable, "I am Jesus, whom you are persecuting" (Acts 9:4–5).

Paul knew Jesus Christ because of his direct encounter with the living Lord. How could he not have had faith? What about a blinding light for us? But we shouldn't assume it was easy under these circumstances for Paul to have faith. He even downplayed his religious experience. In his first letter to the church at Corinth, Paul says the importance of his encounter was not the experience itself, no matter how important it must have been for his life. Rather, the central significance of the encounter on the Damascus road was the sense of calling that came from it. As reported in Acts, he was told "get up and enter the city, and you will be told what you are to do" (Acts 9:6).

Paul's mission was more important than the experience. It would have been nice to have seen what Paul saw on the road to Damascus, but the real issue lies elsewhere. What is to be done with the calling, Paul's calling, our calling? Can we make the leap from spiritual encounter to discipleship that Paul did? Or do we rest in the religious experience as such? Paul rejected that temptation.

In his first letter to the Corinthians, Paul boldly witnessed to the fact that he, like the disciples in the Jerusalem church, had seen the risen Lord. This established his authority and credibility among first-century Christians. However, the encounter on the Damascus road was never described by Paul in his writing. Instead, he spoke constantly of the mission that resulted from his encounter with Christ. This was articulated beautifully in 1 Corinthians 15:8–11:

> Last of all, as to one untimely born, he appeared also to me. For I am the least of the apostles, unfit to be called an apostle, because I persecuted the church of God. But by the grace of God I am what I am, and his grace toward me has not been in vain. On the contrary, I worked harder than any of them—though it was not I, but the grace of God that is with me. Whether then it was I or they, so we proclaim and so you have come to believe.

The mission was all-important to Paul, not he himself. He did not linger on his own experience of Christ.

For Paul, all else was secondary to the proclamation of God's love in Christ Jesus. He committed his life in discipleship. And as we have seen, he was prepared to suffer all hardships for the sake of the gospel. Paul knew his response to God's calling required a faith that only God could give. This kind of faith could not be manufactured; all Paul could do was respond with amazement and gratitude. Perhaps now we know why Paul could say in Romans 8 that nothing can "separate us from the love of God in Christ Jesus." For many, this statement must have appeared as fiction or lunacy. But having walked a distance with Paul, we can say with certainty that he paid the price of his convictions. He lived a life of hope because he had experienced the love of God. And he had passed that love on to the churches. Hope is alive for Paul for the simple and uncomplicated reason that Christ lives—God with us and for us.

Julian of Norwich (c. 1342–1416)

More than a thousand years after the apostle Paul, Dame Julian echoed his hopeful confidence in God's love by declaring "all will be well."[6] She, like Paul, confessed that nothing in all creation can separate us from the love of God. But Julian lived in a very different world from first-century Palestine. She lived and wrote in medieval England. She was a part of what historians call Christendom, a Christianity that dominated culture and church during the European Middle Ages.

Yet, like Paul in the ancient church, Julian had a burning desire to let her world know of God's mercy and grace through Jesus Christ. Her message of God's unconditional love for every person was as unconventional in the fourteenth century as Paul's message was in the first century. Also, like Paul, Julian had the personal courage and spiritual insights that cut through to the heart of faith.

When I first read Julian's *Showings,* her hope-filled account of Christian love, I understood little of it. It struck me as an obscure and distant document of the Middle Ages. Its medieval religiosity turned me off: her report of visions seemed bizarre, and her certainty of God's love was too strong for my sophisticated modern mind. Was this person for real? What could I possibly learn from her? But I persisted in my reading because I knew Dame Julian's writings had spoken directly to the lives of others I admired. (Sometimes mining for gold demands that we dig much deeper than we might prefer.)

I tried to read Julian again; this time with a new set of questions. What prompted Julian to write as she did? What is the significance of the personal revelations that came to her as a young woman upon her deathbed? After recovering from near-death, why did she spend the remainder of her long life trying to grasp the meaning of her youthful visions? Why was she adamant about passing her message on to her contemporaries, and by extension, to you and to me?

With these questions in mind, I returned to the *Showings.* Then came the surprise! The more I meditated on the *Showings,* the more direct and immediate they became. Like all good spiritual writing, Julian's has the uncanny ability to reach across the centuries. I discovered she was trying to tell me something about God and myself. But what? I needed to know more.

In reading Julian, it occurred to me that there is no magic line that divides history between the time when God spoke and when God stopped speaking. Yes, in the Bible, God has spoken to us in a very special way; that is why we set it off as Holy Scripture, as God's Word. But Jesus himself promised that God would continue to speak to us through the Holy Spirit. I wondered if God might not be speaking to me through the life of a medieval woman. Why not? God has spoken to me (to us?) through voices as varied in time as St. Augustine and Desmond Tutu. Why not Julian of Norwich? I had discovered another spiritual partner for silent conversation. With Julian, we have yet another window opened to God.

The Showings

At the age of thirty, Julian fell seriously ill and was given the last rites of the medieval church. She was not expected to live. But she did, and this personal crisis marked the turning point of Julian's life. It was during this time of sickness that she received her revelations. She then recorded these communications from God in a series of writings popularly known today as her *Showings.*

Beyond these writings, however, we know little for certain about Julian. It may be that the name Julian is taken from the church of St. Julian in Norwich, where she attached herself as an anchoress.[7] It was probably after her near-death experience that she became an anchoress, but even this we are not sure of. We do know that during her deathbed experience, while gazing upon a crucifix, Julian had sixteen distinct revelations or visions. These involved the passion of Jesus' death and its meaning for her life. After recovering from her illness, Julian recorded her showings. This was done in two separate pieces of writing divided by some twenty years.

Thus Julian took a lifetime to explore the message of her visions. From the time of her revelations in 1373 (she would have no others) until her death in 1416, Julian examined in prayerful detail the deeper meaning of her visions. By the time she wrote the expanded edition of *Showings* late in her life, she was convinced that her revelations were not private visions. The *Showings* were for the good of others! Julian, humbly and respectfully, came to believe that God was speaking through her to the church and the world. She never understood why that was so, but that it was so she never doubted in her mature years.

According to writer Karen Armstrong, Julian was more like a prophet "who brings a message of God to mankind than a mystic."[8] Like Paul, her calling as God's messenger superseded any fascination she had with her private religious experience. Her writings are marked by the intimacy and spiritual directness we often find in mystics, and her *Showings* should be listed among the classics of Western spirituality. Yet her main emphasis is not inward but outward. She wants to get her message out to a troubled world—a world in need of a good word, in need of hope.

Julian's public mission, however, was complicated by her religious choice of the vocation of an anchoress. She intentionally removed herself from the world. Sometime after her visions, Julian had herself immured in a small apartment adjacent to the cathedral in Norwich and walled off from the world. However, Julian's self-imposed isolation ironically brought her greater, public recognition. Norwich was England's second largest city, and it was of tremendous benefit for the town to add another holy anchoress to its ranks. This added yet another spiritual dimension to its religious relics, pilgrim sites, and grand cathedral. And although cloistered in her apartment, Julian was able to counsel hundreds of spiritual pilgrims who came by her window for advice. Julian could speak God's word like a prophet, but the world must come to her. She could not go to the world.

Armstrong offers an intriguing description of the life of the medieval anchoress. It reminds us how far, in many ways, we are removed from the Middle Ages. In *Visions of God,* Armstrong tells of the anchoress's experience:

> She generally lived in a room next to the church, which had a window in the wall through which she could watch the Mass and receive the sacraments. The anchoress would be interred in the room at an impressive if rather disturbing ceremony during a Mass for the Dead. She would publicly don her religious habit and walk into the cell as into her grave, while the presiding bishop sprinkled ashes in her wake. Henceforth, like St. Paul, she was dead to the world and alive only to God.[9]

This is how it must have been for Julian. Her anchorage exists today in a reconstructed form alongside St. Julian's Cathedral, which was rebuilt after the bombings of World War II.

All Will Be Well

Julian's situation as a prophet behind the walls is somewhat akin to that of her modern-day spiritual counterpart and admirer Thomas Merton. Like Merton, Julian relied upon others to carry her message beyond the confines of her cloistered existence. But unlike Merton, whose writings made him famous in his lifetime, Julian's writings were read by very few in her lifetime. There was no printing press, and literacy was quite low. It was not until the mid-seventeenth century that her *Showings* received even modest circulation.[10] Today, however, her *Showings* are printed in numerous languages and studied by thousands.

What kind of writings are the *Showings?* We should let Julian answer for herself. In its opening pages, she reports to the reader, "These revelations were shown to a simple uneducated creature in the year of our Lord 1373 on 13 May."[11] Julian dates her visions on a precise day in her thirtieth year to remind readers that her revelations don't happen outside of time but in time, and they are meant for those who live in time. At first we may be confused by Julian's claim to be "a simple uneducated creature." Perhaps at the time of her visions, she had not yet received her education. But as an anchoress, she would have had the ability to read and write. Anchoresses generally had to be women of means in order to support their religious way of life. We know, for example, that Julian had two servants named Sara and Alice who did her shopping and errands.[12] Her traditional title of Dame also suggests a social position of rank in Norwich.

Historians continue to speculate about Julian's reference to her uneducated status. Was this a conventional statement of humility, or was it the historical reality at the time of her revelations? In either case, we know that Julian in her mature years could write eloquently. Today she is often recognized as the first great woman writer in the English language. Rather than write in Latin, the official language of her church, she chose the plainer language of her own people. Julian wanted to communicate directly to the inhabitants of Norwich and the surrounding English countryside.

The *Showings* reveal an individual filled with faith. The sixteen different revelations that came to Julian are described in great detail. Awakening from the unconscious state brought about by her illness, Julian wondered if her revelations might have resulted from delirium brought on by sickness. However, after lapsing again into an exhausting sleep, she received a sixteenth and final revelation that reassured her that her awakenings were genuine. In response, she wrote about Christ and the Virgin Mary and the Trinity. But the basic message from Julian's *Showings* is simple: God loves and cares for each of us, and regardless of our circumstances, we are to know that in the end "all will be well."[13]

Set in the context of Julian's day, this is a truly amazing message. The church's theology in the fourteenth century had all but abandoned the world as a vale of tears. Its theology was otherworldly. However, Julian was far more optimistic about life. Her theology was this worldly! God loves us here and now, and if the outcome in the future is to be good, it is because of the nature of God's constant love, not because we have left this world behind. Now is the time of our salvation, writes Julian. Now is the time of hope and faithful expressions of love.

In Julian's time, this was unprecedented Good News! The fourteenth century was ravaged by unending religious wars; Norwich was visited by the plague on several occasions; and the church was torn by various contenders for the papacy. In Western history, no century except the twentieth century has known such a high level of violence and disorder. Yet Julian's writings are filled with hope.

At the close of the "long text" of her *Showings,* Julian reaffirms the central message of her youthful visions. She did this in one word—love. The focus of her *Showings* was God's love for the world as Julian understood this love in and through Jesus. I can imagine Julian sharing this message of God's love with those she counseled from her anchorage window. Recalling her own experience, she offered hope to others:

I desired many times to know in what was our Lord's meaning. And fifteen years after and more, I was answered in spiritual understanding. . . . Know it well, love was his [the Lord's] meaning. Who reveals it to you? Love. What did he reveal to you? Love. Why did he reveal it to you? For love. Remain in this, and you will know more of the same. But you will never know different, without end.[14]

Julian concludes, "So I was taught that love is our Lord's meaning."[15] Her guidance to others was the same as the apostle Paul's: "Make love your aim" (1 Corinthians 14:1, NKJV). In a century of darkness and despair, Julian remained unflappable in her faith concerning God's compassion through Christ. She was convinced that God's love is the only light bright enough to direct us out of darkness. Here was the only true hope. In the sixteenth and final revelation, Julian speaks directly about the illumination of God's love in our lives. In the fullness of her theological understanding, she speaks about the reality of God using both male and female imagery. Her theology remains thoroughly Trinitarian, but its effect is stunning!

Our faith is a light, coming in nature from our endless day, which is our Father, God; in which light our Mother, Christ, and our good Lord the Holy Spirit lead us in this passing life. This light is measured with discretion, and it is present to us in our need in the night. The light is the cause of our life, in which woe we deserve endless reward and thanks from God; for we by his mercy and grace willingly know and believe our light, walking therein wisely and mightily.[16]

Julian knows from her visions and experiences that love has gained the upper hand. This love far outweighs any sin that might otherwise bring us to destruction. Again, like Paul, she realizes that what has been gained in God's love through Christ far surpasses anything that might be lost because of human failings. This includes Adam and Eve's fall from grace (1 Corinthians 15:22). Julian exceeds even Paul's hopeful affirmation that in the second Adam (Christ) we gain more than was ever lost in the first Adam's disobedience.

Julian views God's love as that of the compassionate Father and loving Mother. She has no difficulty speaking of Jesus as Mother, suggesting the deep sense of strength and care that radiated to her from her own experience of the living Christ. Julian's theology is refreshingly free of rigid orthodoxy, but she remains a faithful daughter of the Christian church.

When Julian revisits the Garden of Eden, she adds a new twist to humanity's fall into sin. She tells a story about a master and his servant. According to writer Sheila Upjohn, this story relates both to our beginnings in the garden and our salvation at the cross. In her four-teenth vision, Julian tells us she saw two individuals, one being a Lord and the other a servant. The Lord "sits with dignity, at rest and in peace." The servant, as a good servant, remains alert and eager to do the Lord's bidding.[17] As the story unfolds, the servant is sent on an errand by the Lord. He wants to do well; his only desire is to please his master. In a kind of reversal of Jesus' parable of the prodigal son, the servant rushes off to do the master's business. But unfortunately, as he leaves to accomplish the master's errand, the servant falls into a ditch and is badly hurt. Try as he might, he cannot free himself from the predicament of his accident. He cannot even turn his head to look upon his beloved master's face. He is wedged helplessly in the thickets of the ditch.

Pain and weakness come upon the servant. He almost but not quite forgets the master's mission. Fortunately, the master never loses sight of the good servant. He loves the servant dearly, and their bond is never broken, even though the servant seems hopelessly stuck. Light contin-ues to flow from the master's gaze (God's grace) and casts light upon even the deepest shadows of the gully that entraps the servant.

This remarkable story, told in its medieval imagery, represents the essence of Julian's theology and her hope. As Upjohn notes, this part of Julian's vision departs from the medieval church's theology regarding our fall into sin and Christ's redeeming activity. According to Julian, in our fallenness (the servant in the ditch), our desire is still to please God (to carry out the mission). The fall itself is an accident, not a deliberate act of disobedience. Julian's Adam (the servant) wants more than any-thing to serve God (the master). He did not seek to be disobedient, but in his eagerness to serve he fell into near oblivion.

The servant was unfortunate in his circumstance and even clumsy in his desire to serve, but he didn't act out of a sense of wrongdoing.[18] This means for Julian that our sin, our fallenness, remains real, but we shouldn't dwell on this unfortunate situation. Whether our sin is due to accident, clumsiness, or deliberate disobedience; it really does not mat-ter to Julian. Who can judge motives? All that we know is that we are tangled in the ditch. The real issue for Julian is how to get out of the gully and restore the loving relationship that has been lost between the servant and the master. Deriving a second meaning from the master in the story, Julian also is fully confident that Christ, as a substitute ser-vant, can lift us from the ditch. He comes to our aid and restores us to God's loving presence.

Sin is "behovely," writes Julian. By this she means it is a given—the prevailing state of our present existence. We are separated from God; we are in a situation of alienation. But this condition called sin is far from final, or even normative, for a Christ-like life. Sin has been bested by grace for Julian. Our future need not be defined by our past. In Upjohn's translation of *Showings* we read: "Sin is behovely—it had to be—but all shall be well, and all shall be well, and all manner of things shall be well."[19]

Julian declares that there is nothing in this life or in the life to come that can keep God from loving. The good news is that God's compassion cannot be thwarted forever. In the end God triumphs. It is the nature of love to love—and so it is with God, regardless of our sin and shortcomings. Along with so many saints and sages before her, Julian persists in her faith until she finds the center of life—the love of God. And here she grounds her hope. Sin and suffering may win the day or the century, but love conquers all in the end. In her day, the morality plays of the marketplace and the liturgy of the church may have stressed human sinfulness, but Julian knows of a higher calling to please God and be loved by God, like the servant and master of the story.

Julian, I believe, had discovered the most essential fact of our existence: love. Beyond all messages to the contrary, God is love. This fundamental conviction derived from her *Showings* created in Julian a faith and a hope as unshakable as Paul's. Her visions at times might continue to baffle us, but her message is clear and pure. She has grasped with her heart and mind what we all long to hear and know—that in the end, all will be well!

CHAPTER SEVEN

Paradox in a Manger

> Joseph also went from the town of Nazareth in Galilee
> to Judea, to the city of David called Bethlehem, because
> he was descended from the house and family of David.
> He went to be registered with Mary, to whom he was
> engaged and who was expecting a child. While they
> were there, the time came for her to deliver her child.
> And she gave birth to her firstborn son and wrapped
> him in bands of cloth, and laid him in a manger,
> because there was no place for them in the inn.
>
> LUKE 2:4–7

> She "wrapped him in swaddling clothes, and laid him
> in a manger." Why not a cradle, or a bench, or on
> the ground? Because they had no cradle, bench, table,
> board, nor anything whatever except the manger of the
> oxen. That was the first throne of this King. There in a
> stable, without man or maid, lay the Creator of all the
> world. And there was a maid of fifteen years bringing
> forth her first-born without water, fire, light, or pan, a
> sight for tears! . . . They must have marveled that this
> Child was the Son of God. He was also a real human
> being. Those who say that Mary was not a real mother
> lose all the joy. He was a true Baby, with flesh, blood,
> hands and legs.
>
> MARTIN LUTHER, "A Christmas Sermon"

WHAT NEW CAN BE SAID about the Christmas story? It is known by almost everyone, and yet for me it remains the greatest story ever told. I never tire of preachers each year attempting to draw fresh meaning and new inspiration from the paradox in the manger. Emmanuel—

God with us—but in such an unexpected way! Not born in glory and majesty, but revealed to us in the hiddenness of an obscure birth of a Palestinian Jew in the first century.

Perhaps nothing new can be said, or for that matter needs to be said! How do you improve on this story of stories that defines the central redemptive work of God in the world? What more can be said to readers, who, if they know any part of the New Testament, know this story? The scene of the Christmas crèche is recognized around the world. Indeed, we may be overexposed to the Nativity, if that is possible. But I never tire of revisiting the manger scene. Behind the pageantry of angels, the shepherds, the wise men, and the adoring family lies a tremendous message of hope. It is the biblical hope against hope, a hope filled with irony and paradox.

This kind of hope makes for the true stuff of life, and its natural drama is not lost on the gifted writer of the Gospel of Luke. Nor does its paradoxical message of Christmas escape the late medieval monk and sixteenth-century reformer Martin Luther. In this chapter of our *lectio divina*, we want to return once again to the nativity with the assistance of Luke's Gospel and the writings of Martin Luther. In so doing, we may or may not find something new. But we can all be assured of one thing: we will find something rewarding and hopeful in this ancient story. If we have eyes to see and ears to hear, we will discover once again the hidden glory of Christmas.

Luke the Storyteller

The greatest story ever told is relayed to us by the New Testament's greatest storyteller, the writer of the Gospel of Luke. Jesus' birth narrative is found in the Gospel of Matthew (chapters 1 and 2) and the Gospel of Luke (chapter 2), but I have always preferred the Lukan account for its poetic narrative and its attention to human detail. Matthew's Gospel has much to tell us, especially its emphasis on the significance of Jesus' birth for the Gentile world through the story of the Magi, and its deeply troubling report of Herod's slaughter of the innocents. But for the present, we will follow Luke's amazing story of Jesus' birth, and we will consider this Gospel's proclamation of Christmas hope.

Scholars, we should not be surprised, debate the authorship of Luke's Gospel. This may confuse us since Luke's name has been attached to the third of the canonical Gospels. But among New Testament manuscripts, the heading "according to Luke" is not found in the earliest texts. It was probably added by the early church. According to tradition, Luke was identified as a friend and associate of the apostle Paul. I see no reason to doubt this possibility of authorship. Many scholars would concur, although not all.

What is clear about the Gospel of Luke is that whoever wrote it combined it with the book of Acts to form the finest extended narrative in the New Testament. Luke is a master storyteller, and he provides us with a carefully constructed, highly readable account of the events of earliest Christianity. He covers the time just before Jesus' birth through the spread of early Christianity from Jerusalem to Rome.

We are presented an extraordinary history in Luke-Acts. It is unlike the writing of a modern historian, in which the historian strives for a detached, objective rendering of events. Luke's work is quite the opposite; he is passionate about his storytelling. Luke proclaims as he reports: he wants all the world to know about the saving activity of God in the events of Jesus' life. This is not to say he plays fast and loose with the facts. He is a careful storyteller, and he even seeks to give us "an orderly account," but what an account! On every page of Luke's Gospel, there is a sense of amazement and proclamation of the great things God has done.

Luke's Gospel and the book of Acts are both addressed to someone named Theophilus, which in Greek means "lover of God." This may have been a Roman official to whom Luke was writing to proclaim the good news, or the gospel. Some scholars think that the name is a symbolic title for all readers who might have sympathy with the story. In either case, Luke, in his literary composition, is deeply inspired by God and intends to make a public testimony to the truth that had changed his life. He wrote:

> I too decided, after investigating everything carefully from the very first, to write an orderly account for you, most excellent Theophilus, so that you may know the truth concerning the things about which you have been instructed. (Luke 1:3–4)

I think that Russell Pregeant, a New Testament scholar, has struck the proper note when he concludes, "whether Christian or not, Theophilus was most likely an actual person."[1] There is no reason to think otherwise.

Assuming this possibility, let's imagine that Theophilus has little or no information about the Christian faith. And along with that, let's imagine ourselves reading Luke's account of Jesus' birth, as if for the first time. How might we, like Theophilus, respond to Luke's Christmas story? What are the twists and turns in this Gospel narrative that might surprise us? Spiritually, what might we or Theophilus be expecting from God, and what do we get?

Luke, we notice first of all, spends a great deal of time setting up the story of Jesus' birth. He doesn't rush to the manger in Bethlehem. His is a very carefully crafted story. And it cannot be rushed. According to New Testament scholar R. Alan Culpepper, the events of Luke's story that surround the birth of Jesus "are not a dispensable preamble" to the remainder of Luke's Gospel.[2] These events lead up to Jesus' birth and explain the circumstances of his birth. They are not little extras tacked onto the Gospel about Jesus' public ministry and his death and resurrection, as some scholars suggest. Culpepper argues that the infancy narrative of Jesus (Luke 1:5–2:52) is "actually the Gospel in miniature" and should be considered an opening statement of the major theme that Luke will develop throughout his Gospel and the book of Acts.

This argument I find convincing. In Luke's Christmas story, we are able to anticipate the good news of God's surprising and redemptive activity in Jesus Christ. What could be more central? Luke draws us into his Gospel with not one but two birth announcements. According to Raymond Brown, these "announciations" of the births of John the Baptist and Jesus are intended as two diptychs for Luke's narrative. A diptych is an ancient writing tablet having two hinged leaves, and Luke presents the stories of the births of John the Baptist and Jesus alongside one another like the two leaves of a writing tablet. The hinge that connects these accounts is the mysterious work of God. Luke's drama builds as first of all Zachariah and Elizabeth in old age, much like Abraham and Sarah in Genesis, learn from the angel Gabriel that they will be blessed with a son to be named John. He will be like an ancient prophet, and he will announce the coming of God's anointed one (in Hebrew, *messiah*) who will redeem Israel.

Parallel to this story, the drama is further enhanced as another couple, Mary and Joseph, learn in their betrothal that they too will be blessed with a son who shall be greater even than John—and his name shall be called Jesus. The angel Gabriel announces to Mary that she will bear a child by the power of the Holy Spirit. This is more surprising than the previous announcement. As Raymond Brown states, "Not to aged parents desperate for a child but to a virgin [young woman] who is totally surprised by the idea of conception does the angel Gabriel now come."[3]

By this parallel drama, Luke is able to make his theological point effectively. God is about to do something new and unprecedented! First, his salvation drama suggests continuity with the life of ancient

Israel: God acts once again through the barren womb of Elizabeth as with Sarah. But second, startling discontinuity or newness to God's actions is introduced. God will act through Mary, who has not yet known her husband, and out of virginity not barrenness a messiah will emerge. This birth will benefit not only Israel but also the entire world. Furthermore, Mary will be an active agent, not a passive bystander. As she courageously declares in Luke's account: "Here I am, the servant of the Lord, let it be with me according to your word" (Luke 1:38).

The remarkable role played by Mary, a young woman of fourteen to sixteen years of age, is further amplified by Luke. She goes to visit her relative Elizabeth, who is also pregnant, and tells her what has taken place in her life. After Elizabeth's child leaps for joy in her womb, Mary proclaims the Magnificat. In Luke's Gospel, Mary is the first person to proclaim the good news of God's redemptive activity through her son, Jesus. She is Christianity's first preacher.

> My soul magnifies [Magnificat] the Lord,
>   and my spirit rejoices in God my Savior,
> for he has looked with favor on the lowliness of his servant.
> LUKE 1:47–48

Mary speaks of the new action God will take. In the most radical statement of the New Testament, she declares that God will turn the world upside down through Jesus. Picturing the results, she says:

> He has shown strength with his arm;
>   he has scattered the proud in the thoughts of their hearts.
> He has brought down the powerful from their thrones,
>   and lifted up the lowly;
> he has filled the hungry with good things,
>   and sent the rich away empty.
> LUKE 1:51–53

Mary's Magnificat, patterned after Hannah's song in 1 Samuel 2:1–10, fully anticipates the gospel message of Jesus. Luke's Mary, along with Elizabeth, foreshadow the active discipleship of the women and men who will follow Jesus. Redemption is coming. The world is about to see things and hear things it has never experienced before. To reverse a well-known saying, all heaven (not hell) was about to break loose! Yet, with all this excitement in the drama, Luke remains focused on the one true miracle of Christmas. Everything points to the Christ child in the manger. God, and coworkers for salvation like Elizabeth and Mary, make ready for the greatest miracle of all, the birth of Jesus, the very Son of God.

Born in a Manger

Luke sets the time of Jesus' birth during a worldwide census under the reign of Caesar Augustus when Quirinius was governor of Syria, an eastern province of the Roman Empire that included Palestine. This dating presents several historical problems for scholars. According to Raymond Brown, there never was a census of the whole Rome Empire under Caesar Augustus. There were, however, regional censuses taken. However, "the census of Jordan (not of Galilee) under Quirinius, the governor of Syria, took place in A.D. 6–7, probably at least ten years too late for the birth of Jesus."[4] Was Luke distorting the facts, purposely giving us a false dating?

Writing several decades after the life of Jesus, Luke wanted to stress an important theological point. Although he may have confused some of the historical facts, he was certain of Jesus' historic significance. Therefore, he associated Jesus' birth with a decree from Augustus, Rome's greatest Caesar. He wanted to establish the importance of Jesus' birth in the context of the best-known ruler of the Roman world. Who hadn't heard of Caesar Augustus? In Rome he was worshiped as a divine being. The irony of this is not lost on Luke, and so he proclaims that something much greater than Augustus Caesar and Rome had happened in the birth of Jesus. Now, two millennia later, Luke has proven to be correct in his assessment. Although Jesus never held a public office, or wrote a book, or realized success according to the world's standards, he is fully remembered. More has been said and written about Jesus than any other figure in human history. The Caesars of Rome, though important, cannot make a similar claim.

Luke wanted to proclaim the world's salvation in the birth of Jesus. And he didn't mind pressing the point in his account to Theophilus! He even imitated an imperial proclamation in his report of the angel's announcement of Jesus' birth in Bethlehem. All the stops are pulled out, nothing is held back. "To you is born this day in the city of David a Savior, who is the Messiah, the Lord" (Luke 2:11). As Brown points out, "If Augustus is portrayed in inscriptions as a great savior and benefactor, Luke is portraying Jesus as an even greater one."[5]

The birth of Jesus is therefore pictured in cosmic proportions by Luke. The angelic host in the fields outside Bethlehem represents heaven and earth aglow with the universal significance of this single, solitary birth. The shepherds, like Matthew's magi, bow in adoration upon receiving the good news of the birth. It seems all creation is declaring the glory of the coming of God's Messiah of peace. But there is also another side to the Christmas story. A paradox exists; that is, two seemingly contradicting statements are both held to be true. The Messiah (in Greek, *Christ*) comes in glory, but he also comes in hiddenness. God's action in Jesus' birth is revealed and hidden at the same time.

This is the paradox of the manger. Oddly, the actual birth of Jesus is reported by Luke with a minimum of details. After so much care was given to detail events leading up to the birth, Luke's description of the birth itself is only two verses long:

> While they [Mary and Joseph] were there [in Bethlehem], the time came for her to deliver her child. And she gave birth to her firstborn son and wrapped him in bands of cloth, and laid him in a manger, because there was no place for them in the inn. (Luke 2:6–7)

Centuries later, Martin Luther will note there is something very human and common about these verses, something any mother might recognize: loving care given to the newborn child! But other details are absent. Who was present? Who witnessed the birth of God's Son?

There is no royal birth scene. No attending physicians, midwives, maids, or official witnesses! Only Mary and Joseph. No relatives in waiting, no entourage of curious onlookers wanting to be eyewitnesses to history. In fact, the Christ child, as so often has been preached and sung, had nowhere to lay his head. With no room in the inn, the Messiah is born in a stable. This, at least, is what we deduce. In Luke's brief account, there is no mention of a stable, or barn, or cave (the traditional site of Jesus' birth). R. Alan Culpepper suggests that the inn "may refer to a place where caravaners and pilgrims could spend the night, a guest room in a house (cf. 22:11), or to the sleeping area in a single-room Palestinian peasant home."[6] Whatever the case, the event is filled with irony. Luke emphasizes there was no room in the inn—no room for the one who will make room in his heart for everyone.

The symbol, however, that points most directly to the paradox of disclosure and hiddenness in the nativity is the manger. According to Culpepper, this manger was probably a feeding trough for animals, but sometimes the term also referred to an animal stall. Nothing in Luke's account suggests the humility and poverty of Jesus' birth more than the manger. There is no royal bed, only the commonest of feeding troughs. Here the baby Jesus found his first home. What could be more ironic and paradoxical for this, the greatest story ever told?

Many interpreters of Luke's Gospel have connected the manger of Jesus with the words of the prophet Isaiah. "The ox knows its owner, and the donkey its master's crib; but Israel does not know, my people do not understand" (Isaiah 1:3). The manger, in fact, hides the glory of Christ. But the manger is not the only indicator in Luke that our understanding and faith must be humbled before we can come to the manger of the Christ child. The shepherds rush into Bethlehem to see what God has done. But having visited the manger, the shepherds depart, and we never hear from them again. In Matthew's Gospel, the same is true of the magi. Once the wise men find the Christ child, they depart, and we never hear from them again. Why not? Was the truth of God too subtle, too hidden to sustain the interest of shepherds and wise men? Is it too hidden for us?

Perhaps there is always hiddenness as well as disclosure in God's revelation. It seems that God says to us, so you want to know what is happening? Then, look deep into life. Don't look past life, but look at what is placed before you, in all its glory and all its hiddenness. Look for the uncommon in the very common. Maybe we shouldn't be surprised that Mary, who from the beginning cooperates with the mysterious movement of God, is the only one to appear in both Luke's infancy narrative and in his account of Jesus' public ministry. All others for one reason or another, unknown to us, fade from the scene.

We are told that Mary "ponders" all these things in her heart (Luke 2:19, 51). In our *lectio divina* of the Christmas story, we too need to do some pondering. Maybe this is the only way to come to the truth. Maybe the paradox of the Christ child's hiddenness and disclosure demands of us the kind of faithful hope found in Mary's heart. Pondering opens us to new possibilities, to a God who acts in strange and mysterious ways, often through subtle irony and strange paradox. Our partner for conversation in this chapter, Martin Luther, was a master of irony and paradox, especially when reflecting on the Christmas story.

Martin Luther (1483–1546)

No person in Christian history has loved Christmas more than did Martin Luther. As a sixteenth-century Protestant reformer, he preached often about the birth of Jesus. According to historian Roland Bainton, he delivered between 150 and 200 sermons a year, preaching two to four times on Sundays and several times during the week. In this context, the Christmas theme would have occupied his sermon topics each year from Advent in late November until Epiphany in early January. Thus, over the years, Luther preached literally hundreds of sermons related to Christmas.[7]

Luther seemed to revel in the Christmas theme. Speaking and teaching about the birth of the Christ child was more than a religious obligation for Luther. It was pure, unadulterated joy! He developed many wonderful and provocative sermons about the coming of Christ that are still in print. And they remain remarkably relevant. In some senses,

Luther's own story is a Christmas story—filled with the surprising work of God. We turn now to that story before returning to Luther's own treatment of the nativity.

Hugh T. Kerr, a systematic theologian, has summarized Martin Luther's life (1483–1546) by saying it "was punctuated with continual controversy."[8] Hardly anything in the life of this one-time cloistered Augustinian monk wasn't controversial. We have to wonder how Luther, an individual who originally sought the peace and quiet of a monastery, could get in so much trouble with church authorities. I think the answer to this question involves the Christmas reality of God's doing a new thing. Luther was convinced that the winds of change (the Spirit of God) were moving in his church and society, and he believed that God was doing a new thing in sixteenth-century Germany.

Luther did not, however, arrive at this conclusion all at once. But when he did, European Christianity was to change forever. For better or for worse, depending on whether you were among his supporters or his enemies, Luther was a force to be reckoned with. And his life changed the face of Western Christianity. Luther lived most of his life in north central Germany, far distant from the centers of ecclesiastical and secular power. Yet no corner of Europe was left untouched by his theological writings. Luther gained almost instant fame as Gutenberg's newly invented printing press spread far and wide his attacks upon the papacy and many of its medieval practices.

A son of German peasants, Luther was born and died in Eisleben. His father, because of his success in the mining industry, wanted young Martin to become a lawyer. Luther followed his father's wishes, and after receiving a master of arts degree in 1505 at Erfurt, he prepared to study law. However, this plan changed suddenly on July 2, 1505, when Luther was caught in a fierce thunder and lightning storm. He called upon St. Anna, the patron saint of miners, to save him and swore, "I will become a monk."[9]

Having survived the storm, Luther kept his promise to St. Anna. However, as historian Bernhard Lohse cautions, Luther's decision to become a monk was not simply the result of a single promise. As is true with so many things in our lives, Luther's motives for his action can't be narrowed to one event or explanation. Lohse has observed:

> On the one hand, this oath was not the result of careful consideration but rather slipped out of his mouth in a time of great distress. On the other hand, it was more than merely accidental that Luther made such a promise. He had probably thought of becoming a monk before, even though he had not considered it intensively.[10]

In brief, Martin Luther was a man of his times, and the choice of a monastic life was not out of the ordinary for a man or woman of the late Middle Ages. This was indicative of that age's ever-present question concerning the salvation of the individual soul.

During his monastic years, Luther worried constantly about the state of his soul. He worked hard as a monk to achieve a righteous life before God, but the harder he worked the more he became aware of his sins. Luther was obsessed with his sinfulness. His confessors wearied of his persistent efforts to purge himself of every conceivable sin. Luther never did things by half measures, and he was intense as he searched for relief from his sinfulness. We have probably met people like Luther, people whose intensity seems to suck the life out of us. Martin Luther was like this—and I would guess, was not a pleasant monk to be around!

"How can I find a gracious God?" asked Luther.[11] Above all, Luther feared God was an unforgiving judge who was ready to cast him into hell. He had yet to find the God of Christmas, the forgiving and loving God of the Christ child. He saw only judgment in God, and he could find no mercy. Finally his fellow monks could tolerate Luther no more, and he was sent off for further university studies. Fortunate for his Augustinian brothers, Luther's energies were finally channeled into a productive study of theology. It was during this time that he fell in love with the Bible—not as God's punitive word but as a source of spiritual liberation.

In 1512 Luther received the degree of doctor of theology. He was given a position on the University in Wittenberg faculty, a position he retained for the remainder of his life. He had been ordained to the priesthood in 1507, but teaching was now to be his life's work. This appealed to Luther, and he believed that through teaching he could remain a faithful monk in service of the church. Also, by studying the Bible and Christian tradition, he could find relief from his inner spiritual turmoil. A satisfactory arrangement, or so Luther thought.

Finding a Gracious God

It is said that if we want to know something well we should try to teach it. This was Luther's experience with the Bible, especially his lectures on Romans. In the apostle Paul's letter to the church at Rome, Luther discovered the gracious God for whom he had been searching. He realized that he and the medieval church had gotten the message of salvation turned around. Luther came to understand that salvation is a gift of God. It is not something to be earned, no matter how hard we try; rather, it comes to us as a gift, like the Christ child, and we can either receive it into our hearts or reject it. But we can't earn it.

In his lectures on Romans (1515–1516), Luther argued that we are justified, or made right with God, by faith and not by good works. Faith is gifted to us through God's grace, or loving compassion. Good works on our part have importance, but only as the overflow of our thankful response to God's unmerited love. Good works in and of themselves cannot earn our salvation. Salvation is God's to give or withhold. As sinners, we are wholly dependent of God's forgiveness and mercy. The only way out is through the goodness of God, not our goodness.

The turning point in Luther's reading of Romans came in his meditation on Romans 1:17: "For in it [the gospel] the righteousness of God is revealed through faith for faith; as it is written, 'The one who is righteous will live by faith.'" Luther had been taught in medieval theology that the righteousness referred to in Romans 1:17 was human righteousness, our efforts to get right with God. However, Luther knew from his own struggles that he could never do enough to earn God's forgiveness and mercy. The distance between us and God was too great. But by turning things around, Luther came to understand the righteousness in Romans 1:17 to be God's and not ours. The gospel message is that God reaches out to us in Jesus Christ through his love, his teachings, his healings, his death, and his resurrection. God's righteousness does for us what we cannot do for ourselves. It initiates and establishes a new relationship! And through this we become "new creatures" in Christ—a new creation, a new self.

Luther's subsequent emphasis upon justification by faith through grace created what theologian Philip Watson called a "Copernican revolution in theology." Luther had turned the teaching of the medieval church on its head. Using what later theologians designated as the Protestant principle, Luther questioned the meritorious system of medieval Catholicism that seemed to emphasize human achievement in pursuit of salvation. He called into question the meaning of the sacraments, the monastic vocation of religious orders, the veneration of saints and relics. In Luther's mind, the church of his day gave the false impression that individuals could earn their way to salvation.

The great theologians of Christian tradition, among them Augustine and Thomas Aquinas, had never said that our salvation is dependent upon human achievement. Luther knew this. But on the popular level, the medieval church exploited the idea of earning or even buying salvation. This is what troubled Luther most deeply. And he was most distressed about the practice of raising money through the sale of indulgences. In German lands, the pope had joined forces with powerful church authorities and banking families to broker the sale of indulgences. Indulgences were pieces of parchment sold in the marketplace. Their value rested in their papal sanction to reduce the length of stay in purgatory of departed souls. Purgatory, in the church's teaching, was a place beyond this life of temporary punishment where the soul could continue to be purified and made right for entry into heaven. When the sale of indulgences was promoted near Wittenberg in 1517, Luther was outraged. He considered the crude way in which indulgences were peddled among the people on the city streets as an offense against God and the gospel.

Thus, on October 31, 1517, Martin Luther publicly announced his opposition to this sale of indulgences. According to tradition, Luther posted his ninety-five theses in opposition to the sale of indulgences and other church abuses on the door of the Castle Church at Wittenberg. The Castle Church itself contained many relics that earned for pilgrims meritorious release from purgatory which totaled 1,902,202 years and 270 days.[12] Luther declared an end to all this and argued for a return to the gospel of Christ.

The Protestant Reformation had begun. Luther himself never intended to split Europe into two religious camps, Catholic and Protestant. But his criticisms of the pope and his insistence on salvation by faith alone *(sola fide)* were too much for the medieval church to bear. Add to this Luther's elevation of Bible authority over church authority, and there was no turning back. Luther's emphasis on each individual's right to read and interpret the Bible led to his translation of the Bible into German, the language of his people. Luther couldn't be contained by church authorities. He was expelled from the church and declared a heretic, that is, one who holds wrong views.

Luther was not without his faults. He took up his pen with reckless abandon against those he thought enemies of the gospel. During the Peasants' Revolt in Germany, he wrote in very strong language encouraging German princes to put rebellious peasants to the sword. These were the very peasants who had been motivated by Luther's writing on the freedom of a Christian. Also, when Jews in Germany failed to convert to the new evangelical (Protestant) faith as Luther had anticipated, he called for their persecution. Earlier in 1523 he published *That Jesus Christ Was Born a Jew*. This work revealed a positive attitude toward Jews, and it opened the possibility of a better future for Christian-Jewish relations. But that hope was later shattered when Luther declared religious practices in synagogues were blasphemy and must be stopped by any means necessary.[13] Such remarks cannot be justified or defended, even in their historical context. This is an unredeemed and sinful side of

Luther's personality. Luther continued to need conversion for his heart, completely and without qualification. His prejudices, like ours, are harmful and in need of redemption. Luther's anti-Semitism contributed to the persecution of Jews for centuries to come. According to Luther, we remain sinners throughout our lives. But God can also transform us. We are simultaneously saints and sinners. This is one of Luther's great paradoxes.

At times his advice could be quite simple. When asked by his barber how to pray, Luther responded in a straightforward letter. He told his barber to return to the basics: focus on the Ten Commandments, repeat the Lord's Prayer, and recite the Apostles' Creed. Make a garland, he advised, by finding something of value in each of these teachings for the life of prayer.[14] He told his barber to ask for forgiveness, while never forgetting to praise God. He encouraged prayers for those in need. After praying, seek to help those in need. These are things that Luther felt every Christian could do.

However, Luther was often less direct on the Christian's social ethics. In the politics of the German states, he remained quite conservative once the pope's power and influence were replaced by German rule. His ethics in terms of Christian responsibility to the state were built on Romans 13 and Paul's advice that followers of Jesus be obedient to the ruler of the realm. Luther, for all his discussion of Christian freedom, was not a social or political revolutionary. Centuries later, the Nazis would use Luther's political conservatism to their advantage.

However, on the personal level, Luther could not be more radical. As we shall see, his Christmas sermons bring home to his listeners the significance of Jesus' birth for the present life of the believer. Christmas does not remain in the past for Luther but is an ever-present reality with wide-ranging implications for how the believer should live. Here, perhaps, we catch a glimpse of Luther at his best.

Caring for the Christ Child

Martin Luther doesn't leave the birth of Jesus in the past. In fact, he goes so far as to identify the time of Jesus' birth in the first century with the life of his own German people in the sixteenth century. In one of his many Christmas sermons, Luther speaks directly to his congregation:

> Now the time when Christ should come was one of bitterness and extreme poverty for the Jews. They were a downtrodden people and their lot was pitiable, like ours today so that all might well weep bitterly.[15]

The birth of Jesus, the coming of hope into the world, remained as real for Luther in his day as it was fifteen hundred years earlier. He knew a word of hope was greatly needed in his time. The personal trials and social pressures created by an overbearing church had stretched the German people to their limits. Luther, in his pastoral role, sought to relieve his followers of their spiritual anguish.

Much as in his other work, Luther in his Christmas sermons cuts quickly to the heart of things. He often put aside preliminary accounts surrounding Christ's birth and moved to the manger scene. This for him epitomized the surprising and paradoxical nature of God's salvific actions. He preached to his congregation in very human terms about Mary's plight: "The inn was full. No one would release a room to this pregnant woman. She had to go to a cow stall and there bring forth the Maker of all creatures because nobody would give way."[16]

Luther doesn't miss Luke's irony. God reveals divine love not through power and majesty but in the least expected of places among the meek and lowly. What is known to the poor in their simplicity and powerlessness is hidden from the proud and the powerful. Luther believed that by this single birth God had indeed turned the world upside down.

> When now they were come to Bethlehem, the Evangelist [Luke] says that they were, of all, the lowest and the most despised, and must make way for everyone until they were shoved into a stable to make a common lodging and table with the cattle, while many cutthroats lounged like lords in the inn. They did not recognize what God was doing in the stable. With all their eating, drinking, and finery, God left them empty, and this comfort and treasure was hidden from them.[17]

Luther does not hesitate to ask the difficult question, which is repeated by others down through the ages. Would we have recognized "what God was doing in the stable"? What would have been our response? Luther reminds his congregation "there was the maid of fifteen years bringing forth her first-born son without water, fire, light, or pan, a sight for tears!"[18] Surely we would have helped! It was not so much to ask. We would provide for the baby's most basic human needs. Wouldn't we? Or would we turn our backs to the plight of this poor peasant woman and her child?

Luther, speaking to his gathered congregation, says, "There are many of you in this congregation who think to yourselves: 'If only I had been there! How quick I would have been to help the Baby!' "[19] But Luther himself is not so sure. It is easy to say what we might have done after the fact. It always is. Yet Luther presses the point further. He tells his congregation that they say they would have helped, but would they have? Would we? Luther taunts his listeners:

> Yes, you would! You say that because you know how great Christ is, but if you had been there at that time you would have done none better than the people of Bethlehem. Childish and silly thoughts are these![20]

Luther calls us to account. For the real point is not what we might have done in retrospect but what we are doing today. He challenges his congregation, "Why don't you do it now?" It is a contemporary matter of faith and ethics, this Christmas thing. Luther proclaims, "You have Christ in your neighbor. You ought to serve him, for what you do to your neighbor in need you do to the Lord Christ himself."[21]

The true paradox of Christ's manger for Luther is its application for all seasons. It is a one-time event ever repeated! Each time we approach our neighbor in need, we are approaching the Christ child in the manger. During our lives, we go countless times to Bethlehem. Daily the world's brokenness and poverty confronts us with the baby Jesus. Luther puts it this way, "Let us, then, meditate upon the Nativity just as we see it happening to our own babies. I would not have you contemplate the deity of Christ, the majesty of Christ, but rather his flesh."[22] See Christ in your neighbor!

The Gospel of Luke and the preacher Martin Luther both understood that the good news of Christmas and the Christ child is always present. The hiddenness of God in a manger can be seen—when we see the face of Christ in the neighbor. Christmas comes, as Christ comes to us, in so many different guises. Christ is our barber, our children, our sisters and brothers in the faith, the stranger, the enemy. Christ is the heretic, those we consider unrighteous for whatever reason. God has truly turned the world upside down at the manger and at the cross—more so than even Luther could imagine.

"Christmas comes but once a year" is a maxim only for those who have sealed themselves off from the paradoxical power of the Christ child. Each new day brings another Christmas—this is the sustaining hope of Jesus. Luke and Luther continue to light the Christmas candle in our hearts. Are we able to see the manger and its precious child? We can if we look to the person next to us.

CHAPTER EIGHT

All in the Family

Realizing that their father [Jacob] was dead, Joseph's brothers said, "What if Joseph still bears a grudge against us and pays us back in full for all the wrong that we did to him?" So they approached Joseph, saying, "Your father gave this instruction before he died, 'Say to Joseph: I beg you, forgive the crime of your brothers and the wrong they did in harming you.' Now therefore please forgive the crime of the servants of the God of your father." Joseph wept when they spoke to him. Then his brothers also wept, fell down before him, and said, "We are here as your slaves." But Joseph said to them, "Do not be afraid! Am I in the place of God? Even though you intended to do harm to me, God intended it for good, in order to preserve a numerous people, as he is doing today."

GENESIS 50:15–20

All things work together for good to Joseph, for he loved God. Terrible things happened to him, and wonderful things happened to him, and Joseph grew strong and compassionate, very different as a man from the spoiled bragging brat he had been as a child.

Indeed, his brothers did bow down before him, but that was no longer what was important. What was important was that because Joseph had come to love God in this land of strangers [Egypt], he no longer needed to brag, to thrust himself onto centre stage. He had learned to love.

MADELEINE L'ENGLE, *Sold into Egypt*

JOSEPH WEPT. Joseph's brothers wept. The terrible things that families often do to one another are the source of great sorrow and remorse. Jesus, like the prophets before him, wept over Jerusalem and its families. It seems that from the beginning of Genesis until the conclusion of Revelation, the family of God (all of us) struggles to get along, even at the most basic of levels in family life.

Within our own families, we cannot always decide whether we are friends or foes. We frequently use words in our family situations as clubs to beat on each other. Sometimes we even use our fists or guns. Something has gone wrong. We all sense it. Why can't we just get along? The truth is family feuds have been going on for a very long time. The Bible has examples of some horrendous family battles. In fact, one of the most dysfunctional families I've ever seen is in the book of Genesis. Jacob and his sons can rival any family in history in terms of treachery, deceit, and downright bitterness. But ironically, God chose to work in and through Jacob's brood for the eventual blessing of the human race. This is what Genesis 25–50 tells us. If this is so, could God also be working in and through our imperfect families?

By examining the story of Joseph, Jacob's favored son, we will explore how God enters into an almost unredeemable situation and worked in the life of a family to effect positive change. Madeleine L'Engle, a gifted writer and storyteller, will join us in this exploration. Her own reflections on the story of Joseph make her an excellent silent companion for this part of our *lectio divina*.

Who Was Joseph?

In Genesis 37–50, we have the longest short story, or novella, of the Old Testament. It is referred to by scholars as the Joseph cycle of stories. We have here a series of episodes from the life of Joseph, who is identified in Genesis 37:3 as Jacob's favored son: "Now Israel, [Jacob's new name] loved Joseph more than any other of his children, because he was the son of his old age; and he had made him a long robe with sleeves."

This statement stands at the beginning of the Joseph stories like a huge beacon signaling trouble ahead. It tells us about Jacob's excessive and exclusive love for Joseph, a love that nearly gets Joseph killed by his jealous brothers; it chronicles the unraveling of Jacob's family, and it reports the near dissolution of God's promises made to Joseph's great-grandfather Abraham. We are left to ask ourselves how something as well intended as parental love could be so destructive. The answer contained within Genesis's unfolding narrative is simple and hard to miss: Jacob's love for Joseph was the wrong kind of love.

It was a love of favorites. Most of us have seen such types of love blow up in people's faces. It is a smothering kind of love. Joseph was spoiled by his father. The special garment with its long sleeves (or the coat of many colors) set Joseph apart from his brothers. He was elaborately dressed and marked for distinction. But why? Who was Joseph?

We are told he was a child of Jacob's old age; he was Rachel's son! Jacob, who had inherited the promises of God from his father Isaac and his grandfather Abraham, lived during the second millennium before Jesus' birth near Haran, a site associated with Abraham's early history. God's threefold promise to Abraham had yet to be fulfilled. He had not gained a land, become a nation, or acted as a blessing for others. Yet, in the old ancestral location, Jacob was prospering. As Bernhard W. Anderson describes it, "There, through the providence of Yahweh, not to mention his own shady dealings, Jacob came into the possession of great wealth: two wives (Leah and Rachel), two concubines, eleven sons, numerous servants, and the best portion of Laban's [his father-in-law's] flocks."[1]

Jacob, we are told in Genesis 29, loved Rachel more than Leah. He loved Rachel more than anything! He labored seven years for Rachel's hand in marriage only to be tricked by her father into marrying his elder daughter, Leah. Not to be denied, Jacob worked another seven years for Laban to earn a bride contract with Rachel. However, according to Genesis 29:31, "when the LORD saw that Leah was unloved, he opened her womb; but Rachel was barren."

Eventually Jacob had a total of ten sons, but none by Rachel. Leah, and Rachel's servant Bilhah, and then Leah's servant Zilpah, all had sons to add to Jacob's patrimony. At long last, in Genesis 30:22 we learn, "Then God remembered Rachel, and God heeded her and opened her womb." She bore a son, and declared his name to be Joseph.

After this, Jacob and Laban, and especially Laban's sons, struggle over control of Laban's flocks, and there is a parting of the ways among the families. Jacob departs, and after further disputes with Laban's clan and his own brother Esau, Jacob migrates into the future promised land to places like Shechem and Bethel. During this time of migration, Rachel has a second son. But in the words of Genesis 35:16, "she had hard labor" and died giving birth to Benjamin. Now the sons of Israel (Jacob) were complete at twelve. However, the problems were only beginning.

Joseph, the eldest son of Rachel, was given special treatment by Jacob. It seems Jacob mourned the loss of his beloved Rachel by giving all his attention to Rachel's elder son. From the stories that follow, it is safe to deduce that Jacob loved Joseph too much and his other sons too little.

Exclusive Love

The real problem in Joseph's family was not Jacob's excessive love for Joseph, but his inability to equally love his other sons. Jacob had created an impossible situation for Joseph and Joseph's brothers by his favoritism. His exclusive love of Joseph resulted in great emnity between Joseph and his brothers. How could it have been otherwise?

In Genesis 37 we read that Joseph's brothers had such strong feelings against their seventeen-year-old brother that "they hated him, and could not speak peaceably to him" (Genesis 37:4). Joseph made things worse by giving a bad report to his father regarding some of his brothers. What kind of brother tells on his brothers? Joseph was a tattletale! Furthermore, he had the audacity to tell his brothers about a dream in which he saw his brothers bowing down to him as a servant bows to his master. This Joseph was not an endearing character. His father's exclusive love had spoiled him. In fact, Joseph made it hard for anyone to love him.

Anyone, that is, except for Jacob! Was Jacob so caught up in his grief for Rachel's loss that he didn't see what was happening? Or was he so preoccupied with the business of his clan that he was insensitive to family relationships? Whatever the case, Jacob's crowning of Joseph as his beloved son did his son no favor. We almost feel sorry for Joseph—so spoiled, so arrogant with his brothers, so blind to how his words affected others. Madeleine L'Engle's characterization of Joseph is close to the truth!

> He was a spoiled brat, Joseph, the eleventh brother. Indulged, self-indulgent, selfish. He clung to his father and the women. Whined. Got his own way. If one of the wives said no, another would surely say yes. When he was crossed he wailed that he had no mother. His older brothers took off in the other direction whenever he came around.[2]

It's plain hard to like a kid like Joseph. No wonder his brothers turned from him—and against him. When Jacob sent Joseph to check up on his brothers and the family flocks near Shechem, Joseph willingly obliged his father. (I can imagine that he discharged this task with a zeal reminiscent of the student hall monitors I knew in high school!) The last person the brothers wanted to see coming was Joseph the tattletale sibling. According to the Scriptures, "They saw him from a distance, and before he came near to them, they conspired to kill him" (Genesis 37:18).

Fratricide was the brothers' first thought! Jacob's special and exclusive love of Joseph had fractured the peace *(shalom)* of his family. He had spoiled Joseph to the point that his brothers actually hated him. Joseph's arrogance added to that hatred. And now the brothers were about to kill him, destroying any semblance of well-being in an already strained family situation. There was no love left. All looked hopeless, especially for Joseph.

The Bible's Dysfunctional Family

It has been said that all families are in one way or another dysfunctional. But few murder their own! This is what Jacob's clan was prepared to do. The brothers planned to kill Joseph, throw him in a pit, and report to Jacob that a wild animal had devoured his favorite son. However, one of the brothers, Reuben, argued against murder—not even Joseph deserved this fate! So Reuben convinced his brothers not to spill the blood of a brother but rather to throw him into the pit without water and leave him to die.

Reuben's plan then was to return and rescue Joseph. But before he could, another brother, Judah, helped his brothers find financial gain in Joseph's misfortune. He urged them to sell Joseph into slavery to a caravan of Ishmaelites who were carrying goods down into Egypt. By the time Reuben returned to the pit, his brother Joseph was already on his way to Egypt, where once again he was sold—this time to Potiphar, one of Pharaoh's top officials.

So much for Joseph. The brothers had rid themselves, or so they thought, of the family problem. With a bitter sense of irony, the brothers took Joseph's magnificent robe with the long sleeves and bloodied it with goat's blood. This symbol of Jacob's preferential treatment of Joseph, now bloodied, was used as conclusive evidence that Joseph was indeed dead, supposedly mauled by a wild animal. The brothers had to have known the devastating effect the alleged death of Joseph would have upon Jacob. But they had reached their breaking point, and in return they broke their father's heart. No one in the family could comfort Jacob. Rachel's eldest son was dead. The Bible puts it bluntly: "All his sons and all his daughters sought to comfort him; but he [Jacob] refused to be comforted, and said, 'No, I shall go down to Sheol to my son, mourning'" (Genesis 37:35).

Families can sometimes be brutal to their own members. One misdeed can lead to another until the situation is so grave that there seems to be no reprieve. Words are said that cannot be taken back. Jealousy and mistrust build to a level that submerges any goodwill that remains. Reuben's late-hour effort to save Joseph, as noble as it was, was no match for the years of resentment toward Joseph built up among his brothers. Sometimes we wait until it's too late, and our efforts to save the situation are too little too late.

What, if anything, is redeemable in this particular family situation? Given what the Bible tells us, it appears to be a loveless predicament. Hatred has consumed love. Jacob's family is in disarray, and Jacob himself is too old and too grief stricken to right the course. This dysfunctional family is in a tailspin. Some of us have been in this very situation.

Furthermore, God is nowhere to be found in Genesis 37. It's almost as if the demise of Jacob's family is too painful for God to bear. Remember what is at stake here is not just a family but the family of Abraham, Isaac, and Jacob through whom the threefold promise of God is to be fulfilled. How can any redeemable future be possible with such a fractured family? Love is gone. God is gone. Hope is gone. Had the Joseph cycle of stories ended here, the promises of God would have ended or at least needed a new home, for surely there was no future in this dysfunctional clan.

Thank God for God

Jacob's family was about to self-destruct. Today's family therapist would have helped this out-of-control clan to see the logical consequences of their destructive actions. When Jacob acted as he did in favoritism, when Joseph became the spoiled brat that he was, when the brothers allowed themselves to be consumed by hatred, the collective outcome was predictable—a conflicted family on the brink of annihilation.

Intervention was needed. In this case, nothing short of divine intervention! And so God got involved, in a rather fascinating way. God acted in and through the human characters in the story, not around them or in spite of them. God did not pop into the story like an outside intruder. As we read the Genesis account, we discover that God was there all along, working within the events of the Joseph stories to accomplish a much larger purpose. God never works contrary to the human freedom that is given us. Rather, God waits patiently and painfully for our cooperation, some sign on our part that we are willing to enter the redemptive process, the road to recovery.

Thank God for God, that is, thanks be to a God who cares enough to accompany us in our journey toward a more complete humanity. This is what happens with Joseph. In later Jewish tradition, Joseph is referred to as just (in Hebrew, *tzaddik*). His life comes to epitomize the justice and righteousness of God. In the words of scholar H. Stephen Shoemaker, "he [Joseph] resists temptations, he keeps his word, he administers God's justice, and he is able to show God's own mercy."[3] Can this be our Joseph? What became of the snotty boy whose boasting and self-centeredness brought on the wrath of his brothers? Can a person change that much? God thinks so.

Thanks to the patient workings of God, Joseph over time transformed himself and was transformed. In Genesis 39–50, Joseph the spoiled brat becomes a mature adult. And this transformation is remarkable. The center of Joseph's life shifts from a preoccupation with self to a focus upon the mercies of God. Joseph's family finds restoration, and by it, God's greater purposes are served.

But how did this all come about? We can only summarize the story here. "The Lord was with Joseph" (Genesis 39:2). As a slave of Potiphar in Egypt, he resisted the advances of Potiphar's wife only to find himself thrust into jail due to her false accusations. In jail he befriends the jailers and interprets prisoners' dreams. His ability to interpret dreams for Pharaoh's imprisoned cupbearer leads eventually to his introduction to Pharaoh himself.

Joseph then demonstrates great skill and diplomacy in dealing with Pharaoh's dreams and suggests how Egypt might handle the times of great prosperity and subsequent famine foreshadowed in his dreams. This is followed by a meteoric rise to power by Joseph; he becomes prime minister of Egypt and effectively administers Egypt's years of plenty and famine with wisdom and justice.

Could this all have happened? There are undoubtedly elements of legend and creative storytelling in the Bible's account. But the core elements of the story, according to Bernard W. Anderson, are plausible. They fit within a general pattern of Egyptian history with its cyclical periods of famines and its history of rule and influence from non-Egyptians. However, the central truth of the story lies elsewhere.

Joseph is in a position to rescue his own family from starvation, and perhaps even more important, bring about reconciliation. His personal reversal of fortune becomes the salvation of his own family. When Jacob sends his sons down into Egypt for help from the famine, only Benjamin, Rachel's youngest, is kept behind by the patriarch, who is still grieving for the loss of Rachel and Joseph. In a climactic episode, Joseph recognizes his brothers, but they do not recognize him. Rather than immediately identifying himself, Joseph sets about trying to reunite his family and heal old wounds.

Is this the way God works? Sometimes in hiddenness, behind the scenes. Perhaps this is what the Bible wants to convey to us. Out of compassion, Joseph persists until at last his family—including Jacob and Benjamin—are safe and together in Egypt. What changed Joseph? Why was he now compassionate, merciful, and not vindictive? The answer can be found within the story itself.

Joseph, at one point in the narrative, insists that his brothers return to Egypt a second time with their brother Benjamin. This prompts an anguished conversation among the brothers, who did not yet know Joseph's true identity. They feared that bringing Benjamin from Jacob's side would further devastate, and possibly kill, the aging patriarch. They recognized that the sins of their past were catching up to them.

> They said to one another, "Alas, we are paying the penalty for what we did to our brother; we saw his anguish when he pleaded with us, but we would not listen. That is why this anguish has come upon us." Then Reuben answered them, "Did I not tell you not to wrong the boy? But you would not listen. So now there comes a reckoning for his blood." They did not know that Joseph understood them, since he spoke with them through an interpreter. He turned away from them and wept. (Genesis 42: 21–24)

The remorse of Joseph's brothers softened his heart. He was now hearing what should have been said so many years before. Joseph was ready to forgive; the brothers were ready to repent. They each recognized their responsibilities for the family mess. Even Jacob at home, deep down, knew that his prolonged grieving had shielded him from facing his own parental shortcomings. Jacob's favoritism, Joseph's arrogance, the brothers' jealousy—all contributed.

And now all must forgive. Why do families wait so long to say the words that can lead to healing? When Joseph finally revealed himself to his brothers, he said the words that needed to be said. Here, within Joseph's transformation in love, was the word of the Lord.

> He said, "I am your brother, Joseph, whom you sold into Egypt. And now do not be distressed, or angry with yourselves, because you sold me here; for God sent me before you to preserve life." (Genesis 45:4–5)

This is a wonderful story of how God works in us and through us for the preservation and renewal of life. As we shall soon see, Madeleine L'Engle's reading of the Bible helps to open for us the fuller implications of this life-affirming word in the Joseph saga.

Madeleine L'Engle (1918–)

Madeleine L'Engle has been a professional writer for more than fifty years. Many of this American writer's books are internationally known and celebrated. *A Wrinkle in Time* won the Newbery Medal, and *A Swiftly Turning Planet* received the American Book Award. However, it is L'Engle's *Genesis Trilogy* that makes her an especially good partner for our conversations regarding the biblical Joseph. This trilogy includes *And It Was Good: Reflections on Beginnings* (1983), *Journeys with Jacob* (1986), and *Sold into Egypt: Joseph's Journey into Human Being* (1989).

Carole F. Chase, who has written about Madeleine L'Engle's own spiritual journey, refers to her as a "Suncatcher." She says of L'Engle:

> I am convinced that the gift of Madeleine's writing is to catch the Light and make it visible for her readers, pointing them beyond her words, beyond Madeleine L'Engle herself, to the realm of the numinous, to the Creator God she worships and seeks to serve.[5]

The "Light" that L'Engle catches in her writing is love, and its source is God. She seldom if ever hits the reader over the head with God talk. But whether we are reading her fiction, her fantasy, her poetry, or her reflections on Scripture, there is never a page that doesn't reflect the love of God that has illuminated L'Engle's own life and her reading of the Bible.

Madeleine L'Engle has a clear idea about what the Bible is not and what it is. "The Bible," she declares, "is not objective." Why do people treat it as such, she wonders? "Its stories are passionate, searching for truth (rather than fact), and searching most deeply in story."[6] A lifetime of reading the Bible has convinced L'Engle that we do Scripture a disservice when we reduce its contents to only a simple literal level. In *The Rock That Is Higher*, she asks:

> How can we understand in terms of literalism the glory of the Creation of the universe, Jonah in the belly of the large fish, Daniel in the lion's den, or angels coming to unsuspecting, ordinary people and crying out, "Fear not!"[7]

There is something about the Light that resists being trapped in a box—anybody's box. According to Carole Chase, "Madeleine views a literal interpretation of the Bible as an attempt to tame the wild and wonderful essential biblical story."[8]

Does this open the door for interpreting the Bible in anyway we choose? Certainly not. For L'Engle, the Bible has to be viewed in its many historical, cultural, and religious contexts. Its truths cannot be manufactured out of thin air. Beyond this, from a spiritual perspective, the Bible should be read over and over again, each time waiting upon the Word of God that comes to us through the words of Scripture. Quite often, this Word is conveyed in story.

God must love a good story! So many are found in the Bible—filled with imperfect human beings encountering divine surprises. In this regard, L'Engle has an acute sense of the power of these stories. She finds God's light and love shining through the most unlikely accounts of human drama. Which, of course, brings us back to the remarkable story of Joseph. L'Engle summarizes in a few sentences the biblical truth of the Joseph story which we have spent pages exploring and probing. She states this truth with wonderful insight and clarity:

> Joseph was forced to look low for the Creator, dumped into a pit, sold to strangers, sold again in Egypt, thrown into prison, catapulted into powers. And with each strange reversal he grew, grew into a human being. . . . To be a human being is to know clearly that any-thing good we do is sheer gift of grace, the God's image in us shines so brightly that its light is visible.[9]

L'Engle herself has known what it is like "to look low for the Cre-ator." In some sense, she has been where Joseph had been. Perhaps we too know, at least in part, what it is like to be forced low to look for God?

Travels with Joseph

Like the biblical Joseph, Madeleine L'Engle was born to older parents, Madeleine and Charles Camp. Unlike Joseph, she was an only child. The year was 1918 and the Great War had ended, but not before Madeleine's father's health had been ruined by mustard gas in the trenches of the western front. After the war, Madeleine's father did his best to provide for his small family by writing reviews of plays and con-certs. However, his physical health continued to deteriorate until his death in Madeleine's seventeenth year.

Madeleine L'Engle wrote her first story at the age of five, and she has been writing ever since. There have been, however, numerous low points along the way. The decline in income due to her father's failing health forced the family to live abroad in Switzerland where the air was cleaner and the cost of living lower. Placed in an English boarding school in Switzerland, Madeleine wrote extensively in her journals as a way to cope with the school's strict Anglican rules of behavior and with her own lone-liness. It was not exactly Joseph's enslavement, but Madeleine from an early age knew what it was like to live a life brought low.

Returning to the United States, L'Engle completed her high school education at a private academy and then attended Smith College, major-ing in English and graduating with honors. While working as an actor in small parts on the New York stage in order to support her writing,

Madeleine met and married actor Hugh Franklin in 1946. In that same year, her second book, *Ilsa,* was published—the first having been published in 1945. It met with moderate success.

In the early 1950s Hugh Franklin left acting, and the family (one child, Josephine) moved to Crosswicks, an old home they had earlier purchased in Connecticut. There they bought a country store and tried to make a go of it. The family grew; a son, Bion, was born in 1952, and Maria arrived in 1957. (She was the orphaned child of the Franklins' best friends.) Life was difficult during these years—financial stress and growing pains within the family called forth all the family's collective energy.

During this time, Madeleine continued to write but could not get her work published. She all but quit writing. According to Carole Chase's biography: "On the day Madeleine decided to stop writing, she covered her typewriter and walked around it, weeping. As she wept, she found herself mentally working on a new story about failure."[10] Three years afterwards, it was published as *Meet the Austins* (1960).

Madeleine wept, just as Joseph had wept. Just as we all weep from time to time. Circumstances are often different, for us and for our families, and the tears do come. Nonetheless, good things also happen, often when we least expect them, when we seem to be at the end of our proverbial rope. Could this be a propitious time for the movement of God in our lives? Not against us, but for us and with us. Is what Joseph tells his brothers possibly true? "Even though you intended to do harm to me, God intended it for good" (Genesis 50:20). The whole world at times may seem to be against us, but not God. God's loving grace somehow shines through.

Joseph thought so, and so does Madeleine L'Engle. The success of *A Wrinkle in Time* (1962) established L'Engle as one of America's finest writers. Through this fictional fantasy in what became her famous time trilogy, L'Engle worked out her own essential theology. According to Chase, L'Engle developed "the core of the beliefs about God, humanity, and the cosmos that she holds today."[11] At the center is L'Engle's emphasis upon love—the love of God that creates, sustains, and renews life. In fact, L'Engle believes that the only thing that can be said with absolute certainty about God is that God is love.

For Madeleine L'Engle, the Creator of galaxies is also the one who loves each of us. Her affirmation is not based on abstract speculation but on the lessons learned from the Bible and from her own life. After about ten years at Crosswicks, the Franklin family returned to New York so that Hugh might continue his acting career. But Madeleine continued to write, receiving numerous honors and recognition. Meanwhile, Hugh Franklin completed a successful, long run as Dr. Charles Tyler in the television daytime series "All My Children." Not long after retirement, Hugh was diagnosed with cancer, and life changed again for Madeleine L'Engle, this time in an irreversible way. Hugh Franklin died in September 1986. Being brought low again, L'Engle wrote *Sold into Egypt*. This, I think, is her best work because in it she struggles to find meaning in the most difficult of her own life experiences, the loss of her husband and life's companion. According to the book's jacket cover,

> Madeleine L'Engle joins Joseph on this journey [into Egypt] as she herself moves through grief. With the loss of her beloved husband, she traverses the barren desert of bereavement. And just as Yahweh was Joseph's strong companion in the desert journey, in the house of Pontiphar, in prison, and in his rise to power, so God was with the author of this book and, she assures us, he will be with us as we, too, move toward the human-ness of true maturity.[12]

Both Joseph and Madeleine L'Engle moved via their experiences, and their responses to these experiences, toward a greater humanness. They were aided in this movement to maturity by glimpses of a more encompassing reality, the providence of God.

Providence

Seldom do we get a clear picture of what is happening in our lives. We are so close to events that gaining useful perspective remains a constant challenge. Even in the best of situations, our viewpoint is our viewpoint. How do we step beyond the present moment, the present crisis, the current pressing matter to gain insight? Theologians, down through the centuries, have proposed one possible solution—attentiveness to the providence of God.

By God's providence we mean the sustaining and governing care of God. This care includes the vastness of galaxies and our own little lives. Impossible, we say. How can God look out for everything that happens within billions of human lives when there is an entire universe to run? According to any kind of human logic, this is an impossibility. But perhaps our limited rationality is precisely the problem. "For my thoughts are not your thoughts, nor are your ways my ways, says the Lord" (Isaiah 55:8).

In the story of Joseph, Madeleine L'Engle ponders the thoughts of a maturing Joseph in Egypt. This Joseph has grown into the kind of full humanness that God has intended for us. He is attentive to his family's needs; he shows true strength by extending forgiveness and mercy to his brothers. No need to settle the score—that's a path leading away from God. God's providence suggests another way—the way of love. Madeleine L'Engle has this mature Joseph share the following imaginative soliloquy with her readers. It merits an extended quotation for it reaches for the loving heart of God. Joseph contrasts the God of his ancestors to the sun God of Egypt in this creative rendering:

> The God who showed my great-grandfather Abraham the stars walks with us. That is the difference. The sun god shines with brilliance but does not touch its people. The God of my fathers, of Abraham, Isaac, and Jacob, is with us. When my brothers threw me into the pit, God was there, in the pit with me. When I ruled over Pontiphar's household, God was there in my ruling. When I refused Pontiphar's wife because I would not dishonor my master, God was there in my refusing. When I was in prison, God was in my bondage. In my days of power, God is with me, guiding me.[13]

In retrospect, Joseph views his God as being with him and guiding him every step of the way. This is why he can affirm that God works for good even during his bleakest times.

Madeleine L'Engle's reading of the Genesis story moves us beyond the ancient world of the Bible. She believes we can mature as Joseph did, if we are attentive to God and others, and not self-absorbed. Joseph's affirmation of the providence of God in his life lifts him above his own needs to his family's future, to a more inclusive level. He knows that God's promises to his ancestors cannot ultimately be thwarted. He is confident that all creation will eventually benefit from these blessings.

These are bold claims made in the name of God's love. They come from an individual who, according to Genesis, never directly encounters God. Imagine, God never appears to Joseph! Unlike Abraham, Isaac, and Jacob before him, Joseph receives no word from God. And yet he believes. God appears only once in the Joseph cycle (Genesis 46:1–4) and that time it is to Jacob, not Joseph! As Terence Freithem points out, "The promises seem hidden to ordinary view, Joseph builds no altars and associates with no centers of worship. Yet God is with him, and he is imbued with God's spirit (41:38).[14]

Perhaps this is why I love Joseph so much. For most of his life, he is in the dark. Finally he realizes that all in his family, including himself, have sinned. No one in this story remains innocent. It's a messy situation, but Joseph makes the best of it. He learns more from his mistakes than from his successes. He discovers the providence of God slowly at work, gradually turning what was intended as evil—and was evil— toward the good.

Madeleine L'Engle appreciates this Joseph who can learn and grow. With deft irony, she ends her imagined speech of the mature Joseph with these words:

> Oh, my brothers, I thank you for all that you gave me when you sold me into Egypt. Because of you, it is my riches of understanding that I value, not my palace and my power. . . .
>
> And now my brothers have come, oh my brothers, and now that I love them, and they are freed to love me, joy will come again, and laughter.
>
> And I will praise God.[15]

I wonder if we might reach Joseph's level of humanness and see the larger workings of God's providence within and through the circumstances of our own lives? In the end, after all, it's all in the family—the family of God.

PART THREE

Centering on Love

CHAPTER NINE

Centered in Christ

> Jesus went on with his disciples to the villages of Caesarea Philippi; and on his way he asked his disciples, "Who do people say that I am?" And they answered him, "John the Baptist; and others, Elijah; and still others, one of the prophets." He asked then, "But who do you say that I am?" Peter answered him, "You are the Messiah."
>
> MARK 8:27–29

> What is bothering me incessantly is the question what Christianity really is, or indeed who Christ really is, for us today. The time when people could be told everything by means of words, whether theological or pious, is over, and so is the time of inwardness and conscience—and that means the time of religion in general.
>
> DIETRICH BONHOEFFER,
> *Letters and Papers from Prison*

MEETING JESUS IS LIKE encountering the love of God face to face, and once this encounter occurs, life can never be the same again. This is what the Gospel of Mark and the writings of Dietrich Bonhoeffer profess. They also assert that the only way to come to know Jesus is by following him.

To claim to answer the question of Jesus' identity without entering into discipleship is like claiming to know about being an artist without ever picking up a brush. In a real sense, we must enter into an apprenticeship of love if we are to understand who Jesus is. As Bonhoeffer reminds us, Jesus' initial invitation to his disciples was not to believe in him but to follow him (Mark 1:17).

The implication is clear. We come to know Jesus by joining in his life of compassion. Jesus cannot be understood from a distance. We cannot confess belief in Jesus by holding him at arm's length. Only by entering into Jesus' struggle to demonstrate God's love for humanity can we identify with the *who* of Mark's Gospel and Bonhoeffer's writings.

Ultimately the question of who Jesus is brings us back to ourselves. For in answering this question about Jesus, we are answering a question about our own way of life. Are we prepared to follow Jesus into a life of compassion? Are we willing to be obedient to the law of God's love? Can we in freedom and responsibility take up the cross, not out of obligation, but voluntarily?

These are the kinds of questions that arise from the most basic inquiry of all. "But who do you say that I am?" (Mark 8:29). This is the question that is placed before us in this section of our *lectio divina*. By pressing the issue of Jesus' true identity, we will come very close to God, for Jesus is the compassionate one of God. Both Mark's Gospel and Bonhoeffer's witness are centered in Christ. And at the center of Christ himself is to be found the loving grace of God, a costly grace indeed.

A Gospel with Sharp Edges

Mark is the oldest of the Gospels, and its edges are very sharp, not yet worn by the passage of time. It is also the shortest and most succinct of the New Testament Gospels. There is general agreement that Mark was written sometime between A.D. 60 and 75. Tradition ascribes authorship to Mark, a friend of Peter's identified as the John Mark in Acts whose mother had a home in Jerusalem. He is said to have accompanied Barnabas and Paul on their first missionary journey and may later have been with Peter and Paul in Rome. Scholarly debate continues over whether this particular individual could have been the Gospel's author. However, it is fair to say that the writer of Mark's Gospel was well acquainted with Jesus' life and message. Although probably not an eyewitness, this Gospel's writer faithfully sought to preserve and to spread its good news.

God is constantly at work in this fast-paced Gospel. From its opening lines, "The beginning of the good news of Jesus Christ, the Son of God," to the Roman centurion's pronouncement at the cross of Jesus, "Truly this man was God's Son!" we are encouraged to find God everywhere present in Jesus' life. Within sixteen brief chapters, readable in one sitting, the great news of God's love for us in Jesus Christ is boldly proclaimed. The Gospel of Mark leaves no doubt that salvation has drawn near in Jesus.

This is not to say Jesus' message and identity as God's Messiah is self-evident. In the first seven chapters of Mark, there is great excitement about Jesus' healings and miracles but little understanding as to who Jesus might really be. The crowds were impressed with Jesus as a wonder worker, but they were blind to Jesus' embodiment of the coming kingdom of God's love. Everyone seemed to miss this messianic point. Mark went so far as to report a series of negative judgments about Jesus ("He is beside himself"; "He is possessed by Beelzebub"). The disciples themselves were slow to catch on. It is not until chapter 8 that we have the first real recognition of Jesus as God's Messiah from within his own inner circle of disciples.

The eighth chapter of Mark is the dramatic turning point of the Gospel. In this chapter, Jesus signals to his most trusted disciples the kind of Messiah he is. Raymond Brown says of the eighth chapter, "There, after having been consistently rejected and misunderstood despite all he had said and done, Jesus starts to proclaim the necessity of the suffering, death, and resurrection of the Son of Man in God's plan."[1] Everyone liked the idea of a miracle-working messiah; nobody liked the idea of a suffering messiah. The disciples were not sure that this is what they had signed on for.

Mark's Turning Point

From a strategic point of view, Jesus appears to have blown it. He had the crowds right where he wanted them. They marveled at the miracle of the bread and fish, not once, but twice. He had walked on water and shown God's power over nature. His healings were numerous, and he defied life's greatest enemy, death, by raising a young girl from the dead. This miraculous side of Jesus' witness was a real crowd pleaser. If only he had stuck to the miracles.

But even within the first seven chapters of Mark, there were disturbing glitches in Jesus' ministry. He was not wise in his selection of disciples. His friendships and associations were suspect. Jesus had surrounded himself with a motley crew. They included crude fishermen, a despised tax collector, boisterous hotheads, and one who even betrayed him. In addition, he formed close friendships with women (a public disgrace for a rabbi), and he touched and cleansed lepers while keeping company with prostitutes and Roman officials.

The list goes on. Jesus wasn't everybody's ideal messiah. He failed to meet popular expectations. Nonetheless, impetuous Peter was willing to give Jesus the benefit of the doubt. His ecstatic confession that

Jesus was the Messiah (Mark 8) should not be minimized. Finally, one of Jesus' own answered the only question that really mattered. Peter said quite simply, without qualification, "You are the Messiah" (Mark 8:29).

Then, according to Mark, Jesus "sternly ordered them not to tell anyone about him" (Mark 8:30). Like Peter, we finally think we have it all figured out, only to discover there is more to learn. In Mark 8, Jesus knew there was more that needed saying. The disciples needed further instruction—more dialogue with the teacher. Scholars have referred to Jesus' silencing of Peter as the messianic secret of Mark. Why is Mark's Jesus so reluctant to let the so-called secret out? Why not broadly proclaim his messiahship?

From the perspective of the narrative itself, it appears Jesus wanted to avoid a growing misunderstanding of what messiahship, his anointing by God, was about. Immediately after Peter's profession of Jesus as the Christ (in Hebrew, *messiah*), the Teacher silenced his disciples. Rather then being congratulated for giving the right answer, Peter is humbled, and I suspect angered, by Jesus' response. What does this Jesus want from us? Isn't it enough to call Jesus the Messiah of God! Apparently not.

The nature of the messiahship must be further specified. According to Mark, Jesus "began to teach them that the Son of Man must undergo great suffering, and be rejected by the elders, the chief priests, and the scribes, and be killed, and after three days rise again" (Mark 8:31). And we are told, "He said this quite openly" (Mark 8:32). Peter could not believe his ears. This was not what he and the other disciples had wanted to hear. Nor would it be what we want to hear. Tell us about the glory, Jesus, not about suffering. Peter was so upset by Jesus' statement that he took the Teacher aside and rebuked him. Mark uses strong language to report Peter's harsh words to Jesus. As scholar Pheme Perkins notes, the term "rebuke" (Greek, *epitimao*) is the same word used by Mark to describe Jesus' response to the demons who identified him as Son of God (Mark 1:24–25).[2]

What irony! Jesus rebuked demons for acknowledging him. At the same time, he also rebuked his disciples for their lack of understanding. Then, when Jesus reveals the true nature of his messiahship, he in turn is rebuked by Peter. Rebukes were flying in all directions, but still Jesus' role as messiah needed clarification. Opposition to Jesus was growing in the religious establishment, and his popularity among the crowds as a wonder worker could not last forever. Crowds grow bored. They become fickle. They turn on their heroes.

In Mark 8:34 we read that Jesus "called the crowd with his disciples, and [spoke] to them." If there had been any hesitation by Jesus to go public too soon with his identification as God's Messiah, that time was past. Jesus is now prepared to disclose his understanding of messiahship.

Jesus makes a direct connection between the proclamation of good news (what Peter had just done in his public recognition of Jesus as Messiah) and the costly demands of discipleship (what is required of his followers). Confession and costly grace are inseparably linked together by Jesus. Words and deeds go together. But the crowd and the disciples wanted one without the other; they wanted glory without suffering. For Jesus, however, there is both glory and suffering ahead for his messiahship and his disciples. There was to be a blessing, but not without great cost.

Our discipleship is tied to the type of messiahship Jesus chose. In Mark's Gospel, Jesus puts it this way:

> If any want to become my followers, let them deny themselves and take up their cross and follow me. For those who want to save their life will lose it, and those who lose their life for my sake, and for the sake of the gospel, will save it. For what will it profit them to gain the whole world and forfeit their life? (Mark 8:34–36)

This passage becomes the manifesto for the early church as it seeks to follow Jesus. It is our manifesto as well. Each new generation of Jesus' followers must grapple with the fact that our spiritual commitment begins and ends with Jesus: "If any want to become my followers, let them deny themselves and take up their cross and follow me" (Mark 8:34). The call to discipleship is not an invention of the early church. It is not a theological doctrine. It is Jesus who calls us. It is Jesus who shows us how to love, even unto the cross.

From Miracles to Suffering

There is a distinct shift from miracles to suffering in the second half of the Gospel of Mark. Beginning with Peter's confession, there is a three-fold repetition of the passion predictions (Mark 8:31–32; 9:30–31; 10:32–34).[3] Jesus predicts his own suffering and death, even though the crowds and perhaps the disciples want Jesus to continue his ways as a miracle worker and healer. The people were fed up with heavy-handed religious authorities and repressive military leaders. They liked the way Jesus put religious hypocrites and political functionaries in their place. The common people, and the underclass without any voice, loved this and wanted more.

However, Jesus' messiahship was not about scoring points, although the crowds must have smiled when Jesus outwitted the Pharisees by declaring "The sabbath was made for humankind, and not humankind for the sabbath" (Mark 2:27). They surely took delight when Herod and the Romans could not prevent thousands from gathering in the countryside to hear Jesus teach. In short, Jesus loved the people, and they loved him. There seemed to be no end to his popularity. According to Mark 6:31, after the execution of John the Baptist, the people came out in multitudes to hear a preacher even greater than John. The area surrounding the Sea of Galilee was a hotbed of activity. Mark reports, "As he [Jesus] went ashore, he saw a great crowd; and he had compassion for them, because they were like sheep without a shepherd; and he began to teach them many things" (Mark 6:34).

There was a mutual love affair going on. It was a foretaste of the kingdom of God. There was a tremendous healing not only of bodies but also of souls. God was showing compassion through Jesus. But love exacts a price, for it threatens those who choose hatred and violence. It is also an affront to the prideful and self-righteous. Thus when Jesus sets his face toward Jerusalem, he knew what would come next: "Then he began to teach them that the Son of Man must undergo great suffering" (Mark 8:31).[4]

It is not that God delights in suffering. When Jesus disavowed his popularity as a miracle worker, he was not trying to take all the fun out of life. Quite the contrary was true. Jesus understood that true joy can only be derived from a compassionate life well lived. Suffering cannot be avoided, if love in its unconditional mode is to be embraced. The Jesus of the miracles is attractive but asks nothing of us. This is a Jesus without discipleship, without the cross. This is a Jesus preferred by many, then and now. It has always been so—we avoid the cross, the cost of discipleship. But Mark's Gospel will not permit this to happen. Jesus, as the Son of Man, must suffer and die. In so doing, Jesus is demonstrating the extent to which God will go in order to restore love to the center of our lives.

Jesus makes the free choice to suffer and die as he did. Indeed, Jesus' poignant prayer in the garden at Gethsemane makes little sense if not for his decision: "Abba, Father, for you all things are possible; remove this cup from me; yet, not what I want, but what you want" (Mark 14:36). In the end, Jesus suffers and dies out of loving obedience to what he knows to be the will of God, but it remains his choice, as it remains our choice.

Jesus understood the demands of a compassionate life. He persisted until love was at the center of his identity as God's anointed Messiah.

Suffering couldn't be kept from the redemptive equation. Jesus' followers must also count the cost. To be centered in Jesus is to be centered in God's love, a love that demands everything of us. Marcus Borg, a New Testament scholar, writes that Jesus presents us with a consistent focus upon "the compassion of God" throughout his earthly ministry.[5] While others might concentrate on God's wisdom, or holiness, or righteousness, Jesus kept God's love at the core of everything he said and did.

At the end of his Gospel, the writer of Mark has a Roman centurion declare at Jesus' crucifixion, "Truly this man was God's Son!" (Mark 15:39). Even in death, Jesus projects his ever-present compassion. But such love must continually overcome fear and disbelief. In Mark's account, the women who came to visit the empty tomb are told by a young man dressed in white that Jesus has been resurrected. At this announcement, they fled from the tomb "for terror and amazement had seized them; and they said nothing to anyone, for they were afraid" (Mark 16:8).

We too know what its like to be overcome with fear. Yet God's love prevails. What comes next? While Matthew, Luke, and John tell stories of Jesus' resurrection appearances, Mark ends abruptly. Why does the earliest of the Gospels leave us hanging? Maybe the conclusion of the story of Jesus is up to us. Just as in chapter 8 of Mark's Gospel, we have to answer the question: "But who do you say that I am?" Maybe we are part of Jesus' resurrection story.

Dietrich Bonhoeffer (1906-1945)

Dietrich Bonhoeffer is a part of Jesus' resurrection story. This German pastor and theologian passed through suffering and death in his courageous opposition to Hitler and the Nazis. He fully embraced a costly life of discipleship. His writings were banned in Germany. He was removed from his university position. He was imprisoned. And finally, within weeks of the war's end, he was hanged as a traitor by the Gestapo.

However, Dietrich Bonhoeffer never regretted the path he chose, even when it ended in the hangman's noose. He was determined to walk the path of Christ, to act in compassion and solidarity with victims of Nazi brutality, especially the Jews of Europe. Bonhoeffer challenged an unresponsive church to awaken and meet the evils of a totalitarian regime. Unusual times, he argued, require uncommon responses. He minced no words; the church, he declared, "is not just to bandage the victims under the wheel, but to put a spoke in the wheel itself. Such action would be direct political action."[6]

Bonhoeffer, in the name of Christ, was prepared to "put a spoke in the wheel" of the Nazi regime. He viewed himself as a loyal German citizen and did not relish the thought of being labeled unpatriotic and a traitor to the state. By religious conviction he had pacifist leanings, unusual for German Christians in his day. Before the outbreak of the Second World War, he had arranged a trip to India to meet Mahatma Gandhi. He had hopes of finding clues from Gandhi's nonviolent protest against the British that might inform German disobedience against Hitler. But the war made this trip impossible. With the onset of war, every meaningful avenue of protest seemed to be closed. The question Jesus put to his disciples in Mark 8:29 began to take on greater and greater significance for Bonhoeffer. Christians in Germany had to answer for themselves the same question asked by Jesus of Peter and the other disciples: "But who do you say that I am?" (Mark 8:29). Bonhoeffer reasoned, if Christ is the center, then Hitler cannot be! What was to be done? Bonhoeffer's concern was how to remain faithful to Christ and act responsibly in a time of tyranny and lies.

Christ the Center

In many ways, Bonhoeffer was an unlikely candidate for a costly life of discipleship. Born into an upper-class German family, Bonhoeffer had all the social and cultural advantages of his time. He was one of eight children reared in a happy and secure home; he had the advantages of an excellent education in the finest schools. His father was a noted professor of psychiatry, and his mother was the product of a proud Prussian family whose paternal head had been the chaplain in the court of William II.

The First World War, beginning in his eighth year, interrupted Bonhoeffer's otherwise placid childhood. He saw two of his older brothers march off to war; one returned badly wounded, and the other did not return at all. Living in Berlin, the Bonhoeffer family heard daily reports from the front. Young Dietrich was deeply affected by the war. He later recalled, "Death stood at the door of almost every house."[7] As a result of these early experiences, he had no taste for war, and as we have noted he leaned toward a pacifist position.

Bonhoeffer's religious training was typical of bourgeois families in Germany during the first quarter of the twentieth century. Christian holidays were observed, but beyond that the family rarely attended church. Within the home itself, Bonhoeffer received religious instruction in Lutheran Christianity from his mother. However, when at the age of seventeen Dietrich announced that he would study theology in the university, the entire family was surprised and probably somewhat disappointed. By the age of twenty-one he had completed his doctorate, and he finished the additional work necessary for becoming a university lecturer shortly thereafter.

From all reports, Bonhoeffer was bright and well liked by his peers. He was described by fellow classmates "as capable and assured in manner, stormy in temperament, receptive to new ideas, inclined to indulge in teasing, and endowed with a sharp critical sense, which he was, however, equally prepared to turn towards himself."[8] Yet, during this period, there was little evidence that he was a practicing Christian. Like many of us, he did not pay attention to such matters until he came to a time of personal crisis.

Bonhoeffer never said publicly precisely when this turning point came. But something definitely changed in his life. He met the living Christ; he experienced conversion from an intellectual interest in Christianity to a personal embrace of discipleship in Jesus' name. At some juncture, the faith of the heart had come together with the reason of the mind. Many of us could attest to the power of transformation—or in the language of the church, conversion. It is often difficult to put into words, but something changes within us; we may not know when or how it all happens, but we know things have changed. And for the better! This mystery of conversion is described by Bonhoeffer to his close friend, Elizabeth Sinn, in the winter of 1935–1936. The events he refers to probably took place sometime around 1931. Bonhoeffer writes:

> I hurled myself into my work in an unchristian and an unhumble manner. . . Then something else came along, something which has permanently changed my life and its direction. . . I had often preached, I had seen a lot of the church, I had talked and written about it, but I had not yet become a Christian. (I know that until then I had been using the cause of Jesus Christ to my own advantage. . . .)[9]

What a remarkably honest thing to say! That sort of candor opens the way to new life. Bonhoeffer the theologian had now become Bonhoeffer the Christian.

After becoming a Christian, Bonhoeffer approached his academic work differently. He surprised his students at the University of Berlin by opening his lectures with prayer. He encouraged his students, for the first time, to gather around him for a fellowship of study and prayer.

This broke down the traditional barrier between professor and students. In these small ways, the compassion of Jesus began to be visible in Bonhoeffer's life. According to his good friend and biographer, Eberhard Bethge, it was at this time that Bonhoeffer became more active in the life of the church, which he had already identified as "Christ existing as community." Bethge has reported that "the young theologian engaged himself in a disciplined churchlife which was quite unfamiliar to his family and to his theological teachers."[10]

During this period, Bonhoeffer the Christian also turned his attentions toward the menace of Nazism, which permeated Germany. He believed that the Third Reich, the new thousand years of Aryan domination of the world, was an enemy of Jesus Christ and all that the gospel stood for. Hitler preached hatred, while the message of Christ was love and reconciliation. Bonhoeffer challenged what he called the great masquerade of evil. With the Nazis, evil had disguised itself as goodness and light; it presented itself in the guise of a better tomorrow for Germany.

Bonhoeffer was not deceived. He wrote in 1942, "The great masquerade of evil has played havoc with all our ethical concepts."[11] He told his friends in this secret communiqué that appeals to conscience were of little value when dealing with Hitler. Bonhoeffer realized that the use of reason or moral persuasion was of no consequence for the political philosophy of Nazism. Nonviolent opposition to Hitler by this point appeared to be ineffective and even foolish.

Whatever tactics were to be employed, Bonhoeffer claimed that Hitler must be opposed by Christians from the center of their faith. Followers of Christ must stand and be counted in their opposition to Nazi violence and terror and war making. Bonhoeffer understood what Christians have always known but not always acted upon; namely, that whenever anyone is victimized by another individual or group, then Jesus Christ is victimized. The non-Aryan laws of 1933 compelled Bonhoeffer to speak out early and often against Hitler in the name of Jesus. The Nazis' racist laws led to the definition of Jews as nonpersons in Germany. Bonhoeffer anticipated the deadly implications of these laws and called for the churches of Germany to respond. A spoke must be placed in the wheel of the Nazis' war machine.

In the years preceding the Second World War, Bonhoeffer worked against Hitler's policies through the Confessing Church, an alternative Protestant church structure established to oppose the so-called German Christians who were under Nazi control. Bonhoeffer's opposition to the concept of the Führer led to a ban on his teaching and publishing in Germany. He was harassed by the Gestapo. In fact, he was arrested but not held by the Nazis as early as 1937. During this period, Bonhoeffer had traveled outside of Germany to the United States and had served a German-speaking congregation in London. From every perceptible angle, Bonhoeffer knew that the years ahead would demand that Christians in Germany take up their crosses and follow Jesus (Mark 8:34–38).

In the summer of 1939, just before the start of World War II, Bonhoeffer traveled to the United States for a second time. American friends, fearing for his safety, had arranged for Bonhoeffer to be a visiting professor at Union Seminary in New York City. Many recognized Bonhoeffer's future value as a theologian for the churches of Germany and the worldwide church. He needed to be protected from the Nazis. But within a few days of his arrival in New York, Bonhoeffer knew he belonged back in Germany. His path of compassionate discipleship led him to return immediately to his homeland before the imminent outbreak of war. Bonhoeffer wrote the following words to his good American friend, Reinhold Niebuhr:

> I have made a mistake in coming to America. I must live through this difficult period of our national history with the Christian people of Germany. I will have no right to participate in the reconstruction of Christian life in Germany after the war if I do not share the trials of this time with my people.[12]

As a disciple and follower of Christ, Bonhoeffer painfully acknowledged that this was a cross he must take up. Loving obedience required nothing less. He was not certain what would come next, but he was at peace with his decision.

Costly Grace

During the war years, Bonhoeffer joined in a conspiracy to overthrow Hitler's regime. He had determined that no other course of responsible action remained open within Germany. His entry into the conspiracy was through his brother-in-law, Hans von Dohnanyi, who along with other military and government officials had been plotting the downfall of Hitler from as early as the Munich Conference of 1938. The war changed the nature of the conspiracy, and it buried itself deep within German Military Intelligence (the *Abwehr*), which remained inaccessible to the Gestapo.

Bonhoeffer was enlisted by the Nazi government for service in Military Intelligence. Friends in high places had helped arrange this enlistment. This permitted Bonhoeffer to act as a counterspy for the conspiracy as he traveled to Switzerland and Sweden, both neutral countries, and carried secret messages to the Allies. The conspiracy by 1944 had gained some momentum within Germany's military establishment, but when the conspiracy's secret peace proposal, which included Hitler's arrest and the establishment of a new German government, was not taken seriously by the Allies, support for the conspiracy dwindled.

The conspirators decided on more desperate measures. They planned an attempt on Hitler's life for July 20, 1944. When the attempt failed, the conspiracy's leaders were found out, arrested, and executed.

Bonhoeffer himself had already been imprisoned as an enemy of the state in 1943. Soon he too was linked to the conspiracy, and on April 9, 1945, he was hanged by the Gestapo. An English officer who had been a fellow prisoner with Bonhoeffer said of him, "He was one of the very few persons I have ever met for whom God was real and always near."[13] Bethge provides us with this description of Bonhoeffer's last hours:

> In the grey dawn of that Monday, April 9, there took place at Flossenbürg the execution of those who were not in any circumstances to survive. The camp doctor saw Bonhoeffer kneeling in the preparation cell and praying fervently.[14]

Bonhoeffer, executed within weeks of the war's end, died a lonely and horrible death. His parents and his fiancée were not to learn of his fate until months later. All seemed to be lost. But not from Bonhoeffer's faithful perspective. When he left his cell to be executed, he is reported to have said to a nearby prisoner, "This is the end—but for me, the beginning of life."[15] In loving compassion, he wanted others to know that God's love carries us far beyond this present life to yet new beginnings. Bonhoeffer had done his best to follow after Jesus, "the man for others."[16] He championed the cause of the victims of the Nazis. He chastised the church for its passivity in the face of evil. And when all else failed, he entered the conspiracy. For Bonhoeffer all these actions, even death, were "stations of the road to freedom."[17]

Not long ago I stood before the West Front of Westminster Abbey and viewed the statues of ten twentieth-century martyrs that had recently been unveiled by the archbishop of Canterbury on July 9, 1998. High on the imposing facade in one of ten niches stands the likeness of Dietrich Bonhoeffer. He holds an open Bible in one hand and appears to be preaching. In silence I wondered what he might be saying. Then, it came to me. Above the noise of London's traffic and tourists, I heard Bonhoeffer's often repeated lines from *The Cost of Discipleship*. These words echo the good news of the Gospel of Mark. They speak of God's love in Jesus Christ, a grace that is beyond all measurable value:

Such grace is *costly* because it calls us to follow, and it is grace because it calls us to follow *Jesus Christ*. It is costly because it costs a man his life, and it is grace because it gives a man the only true life. It is costly because it condemns sin, and grace because it justifies the sinner. Above all, it is *costly*, because it cost God the life of his Son. . . .[18]

The call to follow Jesus Christ in any age is the call to discipleship. The compassion of Christ leads us to this path. The question remains: Are we prepared to follow?

CHAPTER TEN

Holy Love, Holy Living

Beloved, let us love one another, because love is from God; everyone who loves is born of God and knows God. Whoever does not love does not know God, for God is love. God's love was revealed among us in this way: God sent his only Son into the world so that we might live through him. In this is love, not that we loved God but that he loved us and sent his Son to be the atoning sacrifice for our sins. Beloved, since God loved us so much, we also ought to love one another. No one has ever seen God; if we love one another, God lives in us, and his love is perfected in us.

1 JOHN 4:7–12

. . . to this day both my brother [Charles] and I maintain—(1) That Christian perfection is that love of God and our neighbor which implies deliverance from *all sin;* (2) that this is received merely *by faith;* (3) that it is given *instantaneously,* in one moment; (4) that we are to expect it, not at death, but *every moment;* that *now* is the accepted time, *now* is the day of this salvation.

JOHN WESLEY, *A Plain Account of Christian Perfection*

THE BOLD CLAIM OF THE EPISTLE of 1 John and the writings of John Wesley is that we should expect to be perfected (or made whole) in love during our own lifetime. Isn't this a bit much? Conventional wisdom says that nothing associated with human life can be deemed perfect. Doesn't this all sound a little self-righteous, or at least, overly optimistic? Not according to the writer of 1 John and John Wesley, that is, if we are careful to note that the perfection mentioned here is not what we do but what God does in us.

We can expect to be perfected in love according to God's grace and mercy. Whatever might this mean in practical terms? What did the New Testament letter of 1 John and the English evangelist John Wesley have in mind when they embraced and proclaimed this great teaching? Certainly we are not speaking of a moral or spiritual perfection—only Jesus was perfect in this sense, and without sin. No, something different is meant here.

Perhaps it has to do with an unsettling question that was part of my ordination vows taken as a young Methodist minister. We ordinands were asked in the Wesleyan tradition: "Are you moving on to perfection?" I knew I could answer this question with integrity only if I placed the emphasis upon "moving on" rather than on "perfection."

We are all, one hopes, being perfected in God's love. Both the writer of 1 John and John Wesley recognized that perfection means maturing into the love of God. This involves a dynamic process and is not a static proposition. In our present *lectio divina,* as we prayerfully consider our spiritual journey, I think there is great value in squarely facing up to this New Testament challenge of perfection. Does God through Christ truly hold before us the genuine possibility of being perfected in love—moving on to perfection? I think God does just that! So did 1 John and John Wesley. Although we may not often, if ever, think about God perfecting something within you, I think it is time we should. After all, God works in very mysterious way, even for the perfection of love within us.

First John: God Is Light

The New Testament writing we call 1 John is filled with light. It contrasts the light of God that comes into the world with the darkness and dimness of the world that we often experience. This light of God has to do with the love of God that comes into the world through Jesus Christ. We are freed and enlightened to love because God first loved us. And Jesus is the unmistakable evidence of that love.

"Beloved, let us love one another, because love is from God" (1 John 4:7). These lines quoted at the beginning of this chapter are among the most familiar lines of the Bible and introduce one of Scripture's most frequently read passages. Top honors for the most frequently quoted New Testament verse, however, would undoubtedly go to the Gospel of John's proclamation that "God so loved the world that he gave his only Son, so that everyone who believes in him may not perish but may have eternal life" (John 3:16).

Not surprisingly, there is a textual connection between these two great passages. Both affirmations come from that part of the ancient church, perhaps in Asia Minor or Syria, that was heavily influenced by the teachings of the apostle John, the beloved disciple of Jesus. The specific relationship between John's Gospel and the letters attributed to John continues to be debated by biblical scholars. But there is common agreement that they are shaped by the same school of Christian teachers. They are Johannine to the core, that is, imprinted by the influence and the spiritual discernment of the apostle John.

A major characteristic of Johannine Christianity is its affirmation that in Jesus Christ the light of God has entered the world in the most brilliant way. The Gospel of John makes it clear in its prologue that Jesus is the Light, the Word (in Greek, *logos*) made flesh among us. And this Word-event brings God's salvation to us in an unprecedented manner. According to John's Gospel, today is the day of our salvation.

Jesus as the Word *(logos)* is divine love incarnate (enfleshed) for our well-being and that of the entire world *(cosmos)*. The letter of 1 John says a similar thing: "In this [the Word-event of Jesus Christ] is love, not that we loved God but that he loved us and sent his Son to be the atoning sacrifice for our sins" (1 John 4:10). God loves us in order that we might in turn be freed (the true meaning of redemption) to love others. The light of God's love is at the heart of Johannine preaching and teaching, whether it be in the Gospel or the letters. In both, Jesus' sacrificial death for us, the ultimate act of love, restores our lives to a proper relationship with God and with our true selves. We are set right and atoned (at-one-ment) with God. The shackles of sin and death are broken, and we are free to love without qualification or restraint of any kind.

Before exploring the depth of this divinely given love, we need to explore a bit further the Johannine use of symbols like light and illumination in proclaiming God's love in Christ. And for this, some further historical background is necessary. Why is there an emphasis upon light and darkness in the Johannine churches of early Christianity?

Christians in the Johannine churches lived under difficult circumstances near the close of the first century when John's Gospel and the letters were written. A shadow seemed to be over these churches because of an internal series of conflicts. Raymond Brown has written, "1 John makes most sense if understood as written in a period following the appearance of the Gospel [John's], when the struggle with the synagogues and 'the Jews' was no longer a major issue."[1] So, this was not the cause of conflict. Neither did the Johannine churches appear to be in immediate danger of persecution from Rome as in the book of

Revelation. But there was some kind internal division in the Johannine churches that was causing great unrest. They were wrestling with conflict within their own fellowship—something that has always caused dark moments among Christians. We need think only of our present church struggles over any number of divisive theological and social issues to appreciate the pain these early Christians must have been going through.

At the center of the Johannine Christian conflict seemed to be differences of views regarding Jesus himself. There was a lack of light and insight among the churches about the very source of light, Jesus Christ. How ironic. In Raymond Brown's words, "a division among Johannine Christians had now occurred, sparked by different views of Jesus."[2] Both sides in the dispute claimed Jesus Christ as the saving Word of God as expressed in the beginning of John's Gospel: "And the Word became flesh and lived among us, and we have seen his glory" (John 1:14). But these two camps of Johannine Christians disagreed about what the Word (Jesus) made flesh meant for their salvation. Once again, in Brown's interpretation, "One group felt his [Jesus'] actions set a moral standard to be followed; the other held that simply believing in the Word was all that mattered, and what Christians did had no more importance than what Jesus did."[3] The issue was not Jesus' saving activity. All in the Johannine churches believed they had received salvation from the remarkable light of God enfleshed in Jesus as the Word *(logos)*. They understood themselves to be living in this marvelous light. However, the writer of 1 John insisted that they not only live in the light but that they must also walk in the light. In other words, they must follow Jesus' example and love one another as they had been loved. This was an essential part of redemption.

Accepting the light of God's love (Jesus) in itself was not sufficient. It was not enough to praise Jesus; he must also be followed in discipleship. Praise of Jesus as God's Word was a meaningless affirmation for the writer of 1 John if there was no commitment to follow in love. For the "elder" who wrote 1 John, there can be no separation of the two—once the light of God's love has fallen upon us, we must also begin to walk in that light. Our spirituality (seeing the light) and our ethics (walking in the light) must go hand in hand.

Thus the author of 1 John argues against those in his churches who believe it is sufficient for salvation simply to profess "Jesus is Lord." These Christians act as if recognizing Jesus Christ as God's light for the world is all they needed to do. They believed that this in itself gave them special status, especially in terms of saving knowledge. First John rejects this brand of Christianity. Later, in the second century, this perspective would be articulated in many forms of Gnostic Christianity and once again rejected by the early church.

But 1 John took another tack and argued for a redemptive love (in Greek, *agape*) that gave definition to saving knowledge (in Greek, *gnosis*). "Beloved, since God loved *(agape)* us so much, we also ought to love *(agape)* one another" (1 John 4:11). To be brought into the Light is to be transformed in love. First John said that we cannot understand God apart from God's love. What we know *(gnosis)* of God is this: "God is love *[agape]*, and those who abide in love *[agape]* abide in God, and God abides in them" (1 John 4:16).

First John: God Is Love

The beginning of 1 John emphasized divine light, but by the middle of the epistle the focus has shifted to divine love. Even at the start of the letter, the references to divine light, as we have seen, are connected to the reality of God's love in Jesus. "This is the message we have heard from him [Jesus] and proclaim to you, that God is light and in him there is no darkness at all" (1 John 1:5). The love of God in Jesus illuminated even the darkest places.

In the third chapter of 1 John we read: "For this is the message you have heard from the beginning, that we should love one another" (1 John 3:11). This love, like the light itself, is from God and is centered in the person and work of Jesus Christ. This shift from light to love is a natural progression from who God in Christ is to what God in Christ does. In the climactic section of the fourth chapter, the full force of this theological connection between light and love is made explicit. "Beloved, since God loved us so much [in Christ Jesus], we also ought to love one another. No one has ever seen God; if we love one another, God lives in us, and his love is perfected in us" (1 John 4:11–12).

Thanks to the life of Jesus we know what God is like even though we have never seen God. And thanks to Jesus, we also know what we can become in our full humanity when God's love "is perfected in us." The beloved writer of 1 John insists that his churches see the light of God's love in Jesus and then walk in that light. Too often, we read 1 John in the abstract as if it is a general essay written without a context. We should remember that the writer of 1 John is addressing a particularly painful division within his own Christian community. Christians within the Johannine churches are not loving one another in the manner that

Jesus had modeled for them in his life and death. They were not show-ing compassion and respect for one another as "children of God." According to Raymond Brown, secessionists within the churches in 1 John were stressing God's light over God's love. Knowledge was being promoted over love. A spiritual elite was developing. In other words, these sisters and brothers in the faith had developed God-consciousness (knowledge of divine light) without experiencing God-conscience (commitment to divine love). They had spirituality but lacked ethics.

But the author of 1 John would not accept this kind of loveless spir-ituality. He writes: "we should believe in the name of his Son Jesus Christ and love one another, just as he has commanded us"(1 John 3:23). The writer of 1 John is especially concerned that those who had the means should help "a brother in need." This may suggest that the secessionists (God-consciousness advocates) as "the wealthier members of the community" had failed to respond to specific, physical needs of the poor in their churches. Some things never seem to change.

We are aware of people who are high on religion but low on ethics. The life of the spirit (spirituality) often gets separated from a life of service (the love ethic). Or the reverse can also be true. But 1 John will not abide this kind of separation within the body of Christ. Again and again he persists—we are able to live in the light and overcome the darkness only by loving God and neighbor!

This is the simple but profound light-love formula of 1 John's mes-sage. In the midst of conflict within his churches, the elder of 1 John will not let his Christian brothers and sisters forget that all is lost if they do not continue to love as God has loved us. With the compassion of a shepherd for his flock, he writes with deep feeling and concern, "Little children, let us love, not in word or speech, but in truth and action" (1 John 3:18). Without love, we are surely only a "noisy gong or a clang-ing cymbal," as the apostle Paul wrote earlier to the churches at Corinth (1 Corinthians 13:1). Setting 1 John alongside Paul's great love chapter in 1 Corinthians 13, we find the same basic message. Unless we act in love, we know not God, and indeed, we don't even know our selves. How shall we walk in love?

Walking in Love

Walking in love requires of us that we return to Jesus. The writer of 1 John is careful to build on the tradition and teachings of Jesus that have been passed down to him from the disciples, most certainly from the apostle John. Once again, it should be emphasized that we are not dealing with an abstract notion of love but with the love of God in

Jesus Christ who has dwelt among us. In a scholarly fashion, C. Clifton Black puts it this way:

> The rhetoric of 1 John "abides" in the speech of the Johannine Jesus, enacting the elder's assurance, "This is the message we have heard from him and proclaim to you" (1 John 1:5a NRSV; cf. John 17:7–8).[4]

Jesus is light for our lives because he is the love of our lives; more to the point, Jesus enlightens our lives with love. He shows us how to love. First John declares, "God is light and in him there is no darkness at all" (1 John 1:5). The writer makes this confident proclamation because of his own experience with Jesus as the living Lord. He knows what it means to be loved, unconditionally accepted by God, and therefore he fears nothing. What is to be feared when God, the very ground of life, is love?

First John's affirmation that we are loved and accepted by God is thoroughly Christ-centered. C. Clifton Black further refines this point with his identification of 1 John's faith as being a "theocentric Christo-centricity." In other words, we live with the assurance of love because of what God has done in and through Jesus for us. He writes:

> For the elder, God is the standard of fidelity, of righteousness (1 John 1:9; 3:7), and of goodness (3 John 11), the agent of forgiveness (1 John 1:9; 2:12) whose essential character is light (1 John 1:5, 7), purity (1 John 3:3), truth (1 John 5:20), and, most especially, pre-venient love (1 John 4:7–12, 16, 19).[5]

It is the action of God that brings Jesus to us as the enfleshment of God's love. And it is specifically in Jesus' love that we come to know God as the true light for our lives. Furthermore, it is God's prevenient love, or anticipatory love, fulfilled in Christ that models for us our own walk in love. Once the light has dawned and we know of God's love for us in Jesus Christ, we are freed to love in the unrestricted way that Jesus did. In fact, we long to love, to walk in the light of Jesus' challenging manner of loving. His love is compelling.

First John teaches that love, as known through Christ, can be perfected in us. He writes, "God lives in us, and his love is perfected in us" (1 John 4:12). This is a bold statement for him to make in the midst of what appeared to be a bitter conflict within his churches. Yet here it is: God lives in us (the Spirit of the living Christ), and because of this, love can be made perfect in us. This statement is not meant to be naively optimistic. First John knows of our human shortcomings, our missing the mark again and again (our sins). "If we say that we have not sinned, we make him [God] a liar, and his word is not in us" (1 John 1:10). The elder knows we cannot bootstrap ourselves out of sin by our own efforts. We have too far to climb to get out of the pit of separation from others and alienation from God that we have dug for ourselves. We need God's help.

First John, speaking the word of God, nonetheless declares that love can be perfected in us. And this possibility of perfection is not in some distant future—either this side of death or the other side—but in the present. John Wesley, in his concept of Christian perfection, will hold a similar view. In 1 John this perfection in love is directly related to the new birth that results from our awakening to the light, Jesus Christ, that has come into the world. The elder of 1 John claims that everyone who loves as a result of this awakening "is born of God and knows God" (1 John 4:7). The characteristics of this love *(agape)* are traced by the writer back to the life of Jesus himself. This kind of love cares for others; we are prepared to suffer for the well being of others, and even die for the good of others. As Jesus taught, "No one has greater love than this, to lay down one's life for one's friends" (John 15:13).

This type of love only matures (in Greek, *teteleiomena*) among followers of Jesus if they truly love one another.[6] The word *matures* used in 1 John 4:12 and elsewhere is most frequently translated as "perfects." Our love matures us, perfects us, because of what God is doing in us. Therefore, perfection of love is possible to the extent that we respond to the Spirit of God within us. We are able in essence to grow up into Christ. The *Analytical Greek Lexicon* perhaps says it best when it uses the phrasing "to be fully developed" for 1 John 4:12 when it says "his [God's] love is perfected in us."[7] That is, God's love is fully developed in us through Christ. We are made whole.

We should expect then in our walk with Jesus to have God's love "fully developed." The author of 1 John says to his churches in conflict: isn't this what God has promised in the new life in Christ? If we are truly called to be "children of God" and not "children of the devil," should we expect anything less? God has given us full ability to love, and with Christ at our side we have the capability of maturing into that love. What is stopping us? What prevents us? With God's grace, we can move toward the loving perfection that God holds before us in Christ Jesus. This is the affirmation of 1 John. It is the same affirmation John Wesley brings to eighteenth-century England. It is the same affirmation that challenges us today.

John Wesley (1703–1791)

From a very early age, the seeds of a perfected love had been planted in John Wesley's heart and mind by his mother, Susanna. The daughter of a prominent nonconformist minister in London, she was capable of arguing points of religion with her highly opinionated husband, a learned high church Anglican priest. Susanna taught her children to speak out and question all manner of things, especially theological doctrine.

John Wesley's childhood therefore was a lively affair in the home of Susanna and Samuel Wesley. One of nineteen children in the family (eight died in infancy), John inherited the names of two brothers who had died before his birth, John and Benjamin. At the age of eight, Wesley narrowly escaped death himself when he was rescued from a burning parsonage. This deliverance was understood by Susanna and her son as a sign of special destiny for Wesley's life.[8]

Educated at Oxford, along with his brother Charles, young John was a serious student with a compulsive disposition. He was determined to make something special of the life that God had spared in the fire. Not content with the academic life, Wesley trained for the ministry and was ordained into the Anglican priesthood. By this time he was in his early thirties, but he still lacked direction. He was uncertain about what God intended for his priesthood. So, along with his brother Charles, he signed on for missionary work in the New World. Their assignment was to assist in England's colonizing efforts in Georgia. Wesley thought that maybe his calling was to bring the gospel to colonists and native peoples. This seemed to fit with the evangelical fervor of his student friends at Oxford. They had helped form a small Christian group known by their critics as "The Holy Club" or "The Bible Moths." Led by John and Charles Wesley, this cadre of pious students was also given the derogatory title of "Methodists" because of their strict requirements of daily Bible devotions and their methodical timetables for prayer.

During these years at Oxford, Wesley became familiar with many of the great English devotional writers. He read with great interest *The Imitation of Christ* by Thomas à Kempis. It appeared as if the seeds of Susanna's early religious training were beginning to grow within Wesley. What she had planted was coming to full flower as Wesley read the New Testament in Greek and studied the writings of the early church fathers of Eastern Christianity: Clement of Alexandria, Gregory of Nyssa, Macarius of Egypt, and others.[9]

In fact, John Wesley was developing into one of the finest theological minds in England. But the formation of the heart was another matter. This Oxford don had intellectualized much of what he read about Christianity without permitting it to get into his inner being. Armed with all this theological knowledge, John Wesley set out for the new world. However, by his own account, Wesley was a miserable failure in Georgia. His preaching and pastoral work was ineffective. His insistence upon strict rules and rigorous piety was a flop. Personally Wesley created a scandal when he refused communion to a woman who had left his company for that of another man.[10] His stay in America became the low point in his life. Now in his middle thirties, he was still a man who had not found himself—or God!

But there are lessons to be learned, even in the bleakest of times. While on shipboard, Wesley had met a group of Moravian Christians (German Pietists). He marveled at their courage during a violent storm on the high seas. They showed no fear for their lives and sang hymns to God, while keeping others, including Wesley, calm during the storm. Wesley earnestly desired the deep faith that these simple Moravians had. He even traveled to their churches in Germany to find out more about their concept of Christian community and its emphasis on small, supportive fellowships. He translated some of their great hymns into English and observed their practical Christian witness through prayer and social relief work. They possessed a religion of the heart and hand as well as the head, something that thus far had eluded Wesley.

Back in London, Wesley had little to show for his life. Reeling from his failure in Georgia, he still hadn't found that special purpose in life for which he believed he had been saved as a child. God's future for Wesley was beyond his comprehension. For well over a decade he had attempted to commit himself in service to God, but he had realized no visible fruits for his labors.

Many of us can identify with Wesley's frustrations. After a youth filled with all kinds of possibilities, the hard reckoning of our middle years can leave us with uncertainty. Will it ever come together for us? This was Wesley's state of mind. Confused. Disappointed. Undecided. Who hasn't been at this place sometime during life? Just when it seemed the darkest, however, things began to turn about for Wesley ever so slightly. It was not one great awakening! But in an almost imperceptible turning, he changed. His heart was "strangely warmed" by the Holy Spirit of God.

In May 1738, Wesley agreed reluctantly to go with his brother to a small group meeting on Altersgate Street in London. Several of his friends, including some Moravians, were gathered there for a Bible study. As someone read from Martin Luther's *Preface to the Romans*, Wesley experienced a startling but subtle change deep within himself. In Wesley's own words:

> About a quarter before nine, while he [the reader] was describing the change which God worked in the heart through faith in Christ, I felt my heart strangely warmed. I felt I did trust in Christ, Christ alone for salvation; and an assurance was given me that he had taken away *my* sins, even *mine,* and saved *me* from the law of sin and death.[11]

The religion of the head and religion of the heart had finally come together for Wesley, not in great public acclaim, but in the quiet of his own soul. Wesley now grasped with his entire being the light and love of God so evident in 1 John and in Romans. Everything that had come before this in his life—his upbringing, his education, his ordination, his successes and failures, his hopes and dreams—seemed like a prelude to this joyful inner moment. Wesley was determined from this point forward to become a Christian "not in name only, but in heart and in life."[12]

John Wesley was convinced that the renewal of Christianity in England and elsewhere depended upon a reformation of life as well as doctrine. As a son of the Reformation, theological doctrines like justification by faith had their place for Wesley, but far more important was the need to understand the gospel as a total way of life. Jesus came to change not only people's minds but also their hearts—from this complete new life all else followed for Wesley. Both head and heart worked together to put Christian hands to work for the glory of God and the service of humanity.

For the next half century, Wesley focused on preaching and teaching nothing but what he believed to be the love of God in Jesus Christ. Emphasizing New Testament texts like 1 John 4:11–12, he repeatedly declared that God first loved us so that we might love others. Knowing God's love for us, we can walk as Jesus walked, and with God's grace, we can love as Jesus loved. Wesley traveled throughout England declaring the good news of the gospel—more than 250,000 miles, mostly on horseback. He preached some forty thousand sermons about God's love, and he invited all those who heard him to respond in love.

John Wesley claimed to be saying nothing new. He presented what for him was a plain account of Christianity. He offered an invitation for all to follow Jesus, especially members of the poor and working classes whom the church had all but ignored and abandoned. Wesley, and his hymn-writing brother Charles, made no distinctions among the individuals to whom they preached. All were equal in the sight of God, churched and unchurched alike. Wesley declared that he had but one essential question to ask of those joining in his emphasis upon an evangelical awakening. "Dost thou love and serve God?" If so, concluded Wesley, "It is enough; I give thee the right hand of fellowship."[13]

The man whose heart was strangely warmed led England into a revival of religion. Wesley professed what he called "spiritual holiness" and sought to spread it across the land. This, he said, entailed nothing more and nothing less than the gospel of God's love. And at its center was the compassion of Jesus. Like the writer of 1 John, Wesley moved his generation toward an awareness of love perfected. Wesley preached:

What *is* religion then? It is easy to answer, if we consult the oracles of God [Scripture]. According to these, it lies in one single point: it is neither more nor less than love. It is the love which "is the fulfilling of the law, the end of the commandment." Religion is the love of God and neighbor; that is, every man [and woman] under heaven.[14]

Holy Living

Wesley taught a "scriptural holiness" and walked a middle ground between religious dogmatism, which insisted upon one way of thinking, and religious enthusiasm, which insisted upon one way of feeling. He combined the religion of the head and heart into a life of holy living, resulting in the religion of the hand. In other words, he preached a religion whose active fruits were compassion and mercy.

Wesley taught that with God's grace believers can engage their heads, hearts, and hands in a daily worship of God and service of neighbor. This type of holy living is to be perfected in love. Christian perfection, in terms of a loving or holy life is not an unrealizable goal but is to be expected in this life with God's help. Wesley never wavered from this teaching, although many misunderstood and criticized his position. Wesley's opponents often thought of his idea of Christian perfection as moral or spiritual perfectionism. But all that Wesley claimed was what Scripture taught him: "God lives in us, and his love is perfected in us" (1 John 4:12). Just as our justification by faith is an act of God's grace, so too our growth in faith, or sanctification, is gifted to us by God.

With God's help (the working of the Holy Spirit), Wesley could see no reason why we should not be moving on toward perfection. With God's assurance of steadfast love, Wesley felt freed to experiment with many innovations in Christian life, or holy living. For example, he preached out of doors among the miners of Bristol. He preached in city streets as people went to and from work. He enlisted lay workers (unordained men and women) to carry on preaching missions and pastoral care among the poor. He organized camp meetings for revivals, established fellowship groups into bands, societies, and circuits—and in the process created what grew to become the Methodist church.

However, Wesley and his followers did not stop with these innovations. They also visited prisons, especially debtors' prisons, and cared for prisoners' families. They built orphanages and schools and spoke out against the ravages of alcohol abuse and the inhumanity of the slave trade. Through such efforts, Christianity once again became a relevant part of life in English society. All this because Wesley genuinely believed that God loves all people regardless of their position or station in life. For Wesley the ground was truly level at the foot of the cross.

Perhaps most instructive for our *lectio divina*, Wesley, in spite of all his preaching, never claimed to have achieved Christian perfection. Neither did his brother Charles, who wrote nearly ten thousand hymns and applied them to his daily life. Wesley wrote in *A Plain Account of Christian Perfection* that he did know a few individuals who had moved on to perfection. But, he asked, what good purpose would it serve to name these persons?[15] The focus should be upon holy living and not upon holy accomplishments. This is the remarkable thing; true saints, if there are such individuals, always point beyond themselves to even great saints, until all eyes are upon Jesus and God.

Even in his old age, John Wesley continued to move on toward perfection. He sought to love God and neighbor in his words and deeds until his dying day. This (along with good genes) accounted for his tremendous vitality. On his seventy-first birthday, he wrote: "How is this, that I find just the same strength as I did 35 years ago? That my sight is considerably better now, and my nerves firmer, than they were then?"[16] Wesley never stopped moving forward physically or spiritually. He strongly believed that care for the body and soul are interrelated. He was an avid reader of works on science and medicine, as well as those on theology. His advice to those in his pastoral care (he claimed the world as his parish) ranged from health care to the management of money. Everything in life had to do with holy living—there was no separation of the sacred from the profane for Wesley. All of life was to be sanctified.

Every day for more than fifty years, Wesley would rise at 4:00 A.M. and preach at 5:00 A.M. This he said was "one of the most healthy exercises in the world." On his eighty-fourth birthday, he did admit to slowing down—he could not run or walk as fast as he once had! "But," he added, "I do not feel any such thing as weariness, whether in travel or preaching."[17]

Those who saw Wesley in his last years remarked on the "extraordinary beauty" of his face, his fresh complexion, and the brightness in his eyes. When he walked the streets with his long white hair flowing, it is said that children would run after him and cling to him. But Wesley was far from being an icon, standing somehow above the fray. He remained feisty to the end, living out his scriptural holiness. The day before his death, Wesley wrote a strident letter to English statesman William Wilberforce encouraging him in his campaign against slavery. Wilberforce had been inspired by Wesley's preaching to oppose the practice of slavery. In one last word, Wesley penned to Wilberforce: "Go in the name of God and the power of his might, till even American slavery, the vilest that ever saw the sun, shall vanish."[18]

Whether he was preaching to miners in the open fields of Bristol or addressing distinguished statesmen, Wesley's commitment to holy living never changed. He brought the whole gospel to the whole world and encouraged all to allow themselves to be perfected in God's love. What lessons might there be in this for each of us? Are we called to move on to holy perfection? The epistle of 1 John and our brother John Wesley think so.

CHAPTER ELEVEN

Divine Discontent

I hate, I despise your festivals,
  and I take no delight in your solemn assemblies.
Even though you offer me your burnt offerings and
  grain offerings,
  I will not accept them;
and the offerings of well-being of your fatted animals
  I will not look upon.
Take away from me the noise of your songs;
  I will not listen to the melody of your harps.
But let justice roll down like waters,
  and righteousness like an ever-flowing stream.

AMOS 5:21–24

It may be that the salvation of the world lies in the
hands of the maladjusted. The challenge to us is to
be maladjusted—as maladjusted as the prophet
Amos, who in the midst of the injustices of his day,
could cry out in the words that echo across the centuries, "Let judgment run down like waters and
righteousness like a mighty stream." . . . as maladjusted as Jesus who could say to the men and women
of his generation, "Love your enemies, bless them
that curse you, do good to them that hate you, and
pray for them that despitefully use you."

MARTIN LUTHER KING JR., *A Testament of Hope*

THE PROPHETS OF GOD challenge us to be maladjusted for the sake of
social justice. Indeed, the love of God and our neighbors is to translate into acts of justice. To live with injustice is to deny the everlasting
love of a merciful God. To live with injustice is to invalidate our worship

and our professed faithfulness to God. To live with injustice is to bring judgment upon ourselves. So say the prophets.

Several millennia ago, Amos spoke out against injustice in the land of ancient Israel. For this he was labeled a malcontent, someone not to be listened to because of his ranting and raving. In the twentieth century, Martin Luther King Jr. spoke out against injustice in a racist America. He too was called a malcontent and accused of being a meddling troublemaker. However, Martin Luther King stood within a proud tradition of prophets reaching back through his own black church to the days of Hebrew prophets like Amos.

In the Hebrew Bible (the Old Testament), the writings of the prophets are one of its three literary divisions: the Torah (teachings), the Prophets, and the Writings. The prophet (in Hebrew, *nabi*) was literally God's "mouthpiece" or messenger. In ancient Israel, this individual held no appointed or inherited office like those of the priest and king. Rather, the prophet was called directly by God from numerous walks of life. The prophet was empowered by the spirit of God to speak "the word of the Lord" to the people. These were the prophet's sole credentials!

This word for the people was often an unpopular teaching. It was like a double-edged sword, speaking of idolatry (running after other gods) and of injustice (mistreating vulnerable members of society). Religion and morality went hand in hand for the biblical prophet. There could be no proper worship of God without the establishment of justice in the land. That is why, as we shall see, Amos criticized Israel's worship so vigorously. It was done apart from justice. "I hate, I despise your festivals, and I take no delight in your solemn assemblies." Worship could proceed in goodness and truth only if justice was permitted to "roll down like waters, and righteouness [another word for justice] like an ever-flowing stream."

What we discover in the teachings of the biblical prophets is that God's love, experienced on the personal level, must be extended to the societal level and find its expression as justice. Justice, in this sense, is love distributed. Love and justice are directly related to one another in the mind of the prophet. Martin Luther King reminds us that this is equally true for Jesus and his teachings.

Our *lectio divina* of Scripture would be incomplete without drawing out the lines connecting love and justice. Amos, a prophet in the eighth century before Christ, will serve as our biblical guide. He will be companioned in our study by Martin Luther King Jr., perhaps the twentieth century's greatest prophet. Together they will help us understand, with heart and mind, why the world's salvation may indeed lie "in the hands of the maladjusted." In the hands of the prophets! In our hands—if we also dare to be maladjusted to injustice.

Go Away, Amos

Our initial response to the witness of the prophet Amos might be, "Go away, Amos." Amos was a troubler of ancient Israel and, if we are honest, he still troubles us. His prophecy is harsh and hard-hitting. Amos pulled no punches; he was direct and relentless in his criticism of Israel, for it had failed to keep God's covenant, and it denied justice to many of its own people.

Amos's message is not good news. In fact, it is very bad news! And nobody likes to receive bad news. But here it is in two brief verses. A true lament and judgment:

> You only have I known
>   of all the families of the earth;
> therefore I will punish you
>   for all your iniquities.
> AMOS 3:2

> The end has come upon my people Israel.
> AMOS 8:2

Speaking the "word of the LORD," Amos loudly laments a relationship (a covenant) that has died. He announces the destruction of Israel. Of all the families of the earth, it was Israel that God had "known" best (in Hebrew, *yada*). And yet the covenant between God and Israel was now broken; the promises to the patriarchs and the teachings of Moses were now buried, dead and gone. There was now no exit for Israel from its pending judgment.

Speaking for God, Amos reminds the people, "I brought you up out of the land of Egypt [under Moses' leadership], and led you forty years in the wilderness, to possess the land of the Amorite [Canaan]" (Amos 2:10). But the prophet's words fell on deaf ears. His listeners repeatedly acted contrary to the covenant. They had been unfaithful to God and unjust in their social relationships. They dishonored God and recriminated themselves.

According to Amos, the people of Israel had passed the point of no return. They had forfeited their covenant with God, and now they must suffer the consequences. From this prophet's perspective, they had brought judgment upon themselves—and not only judgment but also the end. This was indeed bad news, the very worst of news. Oh, Amos, go away . . . go back to where you came from.

The Herdsman from Tekoa

Amos was from the wrong side of the tracks; he was from the wrong country! When Amos presented his prophetic message in the eighth century, the former united kingdom (Israel) of King David and Solomon was only a distant memory. What was ancient Israel had now been divided through civil war into two smaller kingdoms. The kingdom of the north, containing ten of the twelve tribes of Israel, was referred to as Ephraim, and to make matters a little confusing, it was also called Israel. Its ruler during Amos's day was Jeroboam II. The kingdom of the south, the other small kingdom, was named Judah, containing the large tribe of Judah and the much smaller tribe of Benjamin. The southern kingdom had the advantage of having Jerusalem as its political capital and religious center. At its center was the temple of the Lord built by Solomon. Through a line of succession, its ruler in Amos's time was Uzziah, a descendent of King David.

Amos himself was a native of Judah, the southern kingdom. In the book of Amos, we are told that this first of the written prophets came from among the shepherds of Tekoa, a small town near Jerusalem (Amos 1:1). However, as a prophet, he was active in Israel, the northern kingdom. This made Amos an outsider. No wonder Amos was told to go home—he was an intruder and an agitator. Great hostility was directed toward Amos and his message. Several thousand years later, Martin Luther King Jr. was to receive similar treatment. Repeatedly he was told to go home: we can take care of our own problems.

Amos 7:10–15 gives us a clear picture of Amos's precarious position as a prophet. We find in this passage a dramatic confrontation between Amos and Amaziah, the chief priest of Bethel, the royal sanctuary established as a national shrine by Jeroboam I. Amaziah assumes Amos is a professional prophet who is hired to serve the southern kingdom and its political interests. Amaziah warns Amos to return to his own country. But Amos responds that he is not a professional prophet. He is not captive to any king or royal household. His only accountability is to God:

> "I am no prophet, nor a prophet's son; but I am a herdsman, and a dresser of sycamore trees, and the LORD [Yahweh] took me from following the flock, and the LORD said to me, 'Go, prophesy to my people Israel.' " (Amos 7:14–15)

By denying he was a professional prophet, Amos was not rejecting his prophetic calling. Rather, he was distancing himself from cults of prophets who often worked for a royal house and told people, especially kings, what they wanted to hear. Amos had a different word.

Being a prophet often means saying disagreeable things. Prophets seldom win popularity contests. But as Old Testament scholar Donald E. Gowan cautions us, being disagreeable in and of itself is no proof that we are prophets.[1] Just because we stir up trouble does not mean that we are a prophet of God. The test of true prophecy is whether or not justice is sought in faithfulness to God. In the Old Testament, true prophets are those whose words challenge the people to keep God's covenant. Genuine prophets call for the people to seek justice, love kindness, and walk humbly with God (Micah 6:8).

Without question, Amos did find himself as a prophet in the midst of conflict. But like Micah, a fellow eighth-century prophet in Judah, he never lost sight of his prophetic purpose. He was determined to pursue justice out of love for God and God's people. Yes, he was maladjusted, but maladjusted for good reason. He refused all compromise with those who broke the covenant. He hated unfaithfulness, and he despised the gross complicity of Israel in acts of injustice. His anger was very real, but it was a righteous, not self-righteous, indignation. In addition, there was a sadness about Amos. His message was indeed very bad news, and his heart was broken, just like covenant.

The Message

Amos challenged the conventional religious belief of his day. In the northern kingdom as well as in Judah, the concept of the covenant had come to emphasize Israel's spiritual privilege among the nations. Of all the peoples of the earth, Yahweh had chosen Israel for a special relationship. But Amos reminded his listeners that the covenant was a calling to special responsibility, not special privilege. According to the tradition of Moses' teachings, especially honored in the north, the covenant was not an automatic guarantee of God's blessings. It was based on the Ten Commandments, and Amos warned that the people of Israel had forgotten this important connection. The covenant was conditional. "If you obey my voice and keep my covenant, you shall be my treasured possession out of all the peoples" (Exodus 19:5). But Israel was not keeping the conditions of the covenant; they were unfaithful to the laws of Moses.

Therefore, Amos declared the future of Israel to be darkness rather than light. From their logic of special privilege, the people expected prosperity and peace. This was symbolized in the Day of Yahweh. Bernhard W. Anderson tells us that the people celebrated this hope of a grand future in a fall covenant festival. It was believed that this New Year's Day observance on ancient Israel's calendar was a foreshadowing of the great Day of Yahweh, a final, glorious climax in which the blessings of the covenant would fully be realized.[2]

Amos, to the contrary, proclaimed the Day of Yahweh to be a day of judgment and reckoning. This troubled and angered the people of Israel. How dare this foreign prophet denounce their nation's hopes and dreams? Yet, in a stunning reversal, Amos lamented:

Alas for you who desire the day of the LORD [Yahweh]!
    Why do you want the day of the LORD?
It is darkness, not light;
    as if someone fled from a lion,
    and was met by a bear
or went into the house and rested a hand against the wall,
    and was bitten by a snake.
Is not the day of the LORD darkness, not light,
    and gloom with no brightness in it?
AMOS 5:18–20

Amos listed his charges against Israel, but began with charges against other nations. He condemned war atrocities of Israel's neighboring kingdoms and insisted on Yahweh's sovereignty over all nations. All nations were accountable to Israel's God. Indeed, for many of the prophets, the Lord was not a national God but sovereign ruler of the world.

So far, so good! The people of Israel would have approved of Amos's judgment upon their warring neighbors. They would have delighted even more at what came next. Amos condemned Judah, the southern kingdom. Tension between the north and the south had existed ever since the breakup of David and Solomon's united kingdom. Both groups, north and south, believed they had been faithful to the covenant. In the book of Amos, however, we find severe criticism for the people of Judah who reject "the law of the LORD, and have not kept his statutes." Because of this, Amos declares that God will "send a fire on Judah, and it shall devour the strongholds of Jerusalem" (Amos 2:4–5).

Next comes the final blow struck by Amos. Speaking in the northern kingdom, in Israel, he condemns its people for failure to follow the laws of God. With brutal frankness, he hammers away at Israel's iniquities. The population must have recoiled in shock. Amos said Israel was unfair in business practices, mistreated the poor, engaged in sexual immorality, and worshiped falsely (Amos 2:6–8). For these violations of the covenant and more, Israel itself would be destroyed (Amos 2:13–16).

These unfaithful and unjust actions in Israel paralleled for Amos the crimes and false sense of security found in Judah. But Israel was blind to its unfaithfulness. Things had been pretty good for Israel under Jeroboam II. The king had expanded his nation's power and prestige through military successes in Gilead, and the rise of Assyrian power was still on the distant horizon. Economically the nation was prospering. There was a general sense of well-being among Israel's elite and ruling classes. Business was good! How dare Amos upset these days of prosperity with his prophetic criticisms?

Amos refused to back off. He insisted there was something fundamentally wrong in Israel. The chief priest Amaziah, as we noted earlier, told this troubler of Israel to go home, accusing him of high treason and stating that "the land is not able to bear all his words" (Amos 7:10). However, Amos would not leave, and he would not be silenced. Bernhard W. Anderson has cataloged Amos's specific charges against Israel:

> Wealthy merchants, lusting for economic power, were ruthlessly trampling on the heads of the poor and defenseless. Public leaders, reveling in luxury and corrupted by indulgence, were lying on beds of ease. . . . The sophisticated ladies, whom Amos—in the rough language of a herdsman—compares to the fat, sleek cows of Bashan, were selfishly urging their husbands on. Law courts were used to serve the vested interests of the commercial class.[3]

According to Anderson, the religion of the people offered no protest to these social abuses. The nation, in its national religion, piously declared "In God We Trust." This disturbed Amos most deeply. This was the source of God's discontent with Israel. This is what made the prophet Amos a righteous malcontent.

Martin Luther King Jr. (1929-1968)

Martin Luther King Jr. expressed the same outrage at his nation's unfaithfulness to its ideals as did Amos—and for similar reasons. Martin Luther King was a prophet called forth by God in his time and place to witness to the power of love, to witness to the need for justice. America, according to King, was filled with darkness and death rather than light and life, because of its racism and its mistreatment of the poor.

I never met Martin Luther King Jr., but those who did sensed a special contagion of love and justice within his spirit. James Washington, who edited King's writings in *A Testament of Hope*, agrees with King's contemporaries "that some strange providence guided the course of his life."[4] In a note written to me not long before his death, Washington expressed the inspiration he gained from King as he passed it on to me, "May we continue to struggle for a better world of peace and justice and love in the spirit of the prophet Martin."[5]

Martin Luther King Jr. had an enormous effect upon those who knew him and upon untold future generations. When Yolanda King, King's oldest child, spoke at our college, I prepared my then very young son for her visit. I didn't want my children to miss the importance of this memorable moment. I told my little boy about the prophet Martin and all that he has meant to me. As we departed for the gathering my son announced, "We're going to see the queen!" When I told Yolanda King about this, she laughed with delight.

My child's comment spoke the truth far beyond his youthful age. The name of King does indeed suggest royalty, and in Martin's case, it suggests the mantle of prophecy ordained by God. We would do well at this point to review King's biography so that we can gain a better understanding of how and why this modern prophet emerged.

Martin Luther King Jr. was a man who was arrested more than fifteen times; who was jailed and dishonored for his social protests; who was stabbed and bombed out of his home; and who was killed by a cowardly assassin. This prophet who suffered so very much for justice was born in Atlanta, Georgia, on January 15 (now a national holiday in his honor), 1929. His parents were the Reverend Martin Luther King Sr. and Alberta Williams King. Martin was a sensitive and bright child who later reported being reared in a caring home. He advanced quickly in his education and passed a special examination at the age of fifteen for entry into Morehouse College.

Theologian James Cone has observed that Martin Luther King Jr. was greatly shaped by his social location within the black middle class of his Atlanta childhood. In a thoroughly segregated South, King's upbringing in an established "Negro" neighborhood was somewhat insular and protected. Within the scope of his own black world, King was relatively safe and secure as a child. His family was not poor, although they suffered the daily indignities of Jim Crow laws and racial bigotry. King reports he was six years old when he first became conscious of racial discrimination. Later, he notes, as a teenager, he was forced to give up his bus seat to whites and was made to stand for ninety miles on a return trip from a high school debate tournament.[6]

These and similar experiences, though significant and traumatic, were not as devastating as those of other black children in other areas of the rural South and urban North, especially among the underclass. But as a part of the Negro middle class, King was made conscious at an early age of his special responsibilities to change things for the better for African Americans. King's father had a tremendous influence in this regard. King writes:

> From before I was born, my father had refused to ride the city buses, after witnessing a brutal attack on a load of Negro passengers. He had led the fight in Atlanta to equalize teachers' salaries, and had been instrumental in the elimination of jim-crow elevators in the courthouse. As pastor of the Ebenezer Baptist Church . . . he had wielded great influence in the Negro community, and perhaps won the grudging respect of the whites.[7]

Thus, when Martin Luther King Jr. entered Morehouse College, he already knew one prophetic figure—his own father.

At Morehouse, King was to meet another African American prophet, the scholar and teacher Dr. Benjamin E. Mays. King discovered in Mays a free individual. Even though Mays was subjected to the physical and psychological violence of a segregated South, his heart and mind was never imprisoned by white racism. Mays, and others at Morehouse, gave King confidence that truth and justice can win out. Years later in his battle for civil and human rights, King never forgot this early lesson. He understood that something far greater than he was at work in the African American's struggle for freedom. He later preached:

> Truth crushed to earth will rise again. How long? Not long! Because no lie can live forever. How long? Not long! . . . Truth forever on the scaffold, wrong forever on the throne. Yet that scaffold sways the future and behind the dim unknown standeth God within the shadow, keeping watch over his own. How long? Not long! Because the arc of the moral universe is long but it bends toward justice.[8]

Support from his family, his church, and his alma mater gave King the necessary spiritual foundation for striking out into an unfriendly white world. He attended Crozer, a theological seminary in Chester, Pennsylvania. Here he prepared for Christian ministry and graduated at the head of his class from this almost exclusively white Baptist school, now a part of Colgate Rochester Seminary in Rochester, New York. King's seminary professors introduced him to the academic world of theological studies and the social gospel of Walter Rauschenbusch. They saw his potential and encouraged his application to the doctoral program in systematic theology at the School of Theology at Boston University. There he earned his doctoral degree in systematic theology in June 1955. By this time, he had achieved all of his educational goals.

However, two other events occurred in King's graduate school days that were of even greater significance. First, in June 1953, he married

Coretta Scott of Marion, Alabama. They had met in Boston, where she was pursuing graduate work in voice at the New England Conservatory of Music. Coretta Scott King was to become the anchor for the King family both during and after Martin's lifetime. Second, before finishing his dissertation, King, still a doctoral candidate, accepted a call to the historic Dexter Avenue Baptist Church in Montgomery, Alabama.

The decision to go to the Dexter Avenue Baptist Church was difficult for Martin and Coretta. With his life in the North, Martin had thought, "I have a chance to escape from the long night of segregation. Can I return to a society that condones a system I have abhorred since childhood?" Like Amos, King must have wondered if God was truly calling him into that country. But Martin and Coretta concluded, "The South, after all, was our home. Despite its shortcomings we loved it as home, and had a real desire to do something about the problems that we had felt so keenly as youngsters."[9] Unlike Amos at this point, and more like Jesus, King was soon to find out that a prophet is not welcome in his own country.

Montgomery to Memphis

Within months of his arrival at Dexter Avenue in Montgomery, King was thrust into the center of crisis and national attention. Mrs. Rosa Parks, a forty-two-year-old black seamstress, took a simple action that challenged Jim Crow laws in Alabama. She refused to give up her seat on a public bus to a white man. Her no to racial segregation and discrimination rocked the South. She was tired after a hard day's work, and enough was enough. She wouldn't give up her seat; she would not be moved! In James Washington's words, "Rosa Parks was saying no to an age of white terrorism that sought to dominate and control African Americans by lynchings."[10] Rosa Parks would not be intimidated by this history.

What Rosa Parks did took tremendous courage. Ever since the period of Reconstruction after the Civil War, white racists had spread fear among blacks and taken the vote away from African Americans by all manner of illegal means. Lynching and burning were a common legacy of this terrorism. In Rosa Park's day, the Reverend George W. Lee had been lynched in Mississippi for attempting to register to vote. Lamar Smith had also been hanged illegally in Mississippi. And most infamous of all, fourteen-year-old Emmett Till was lynched in Money, Mississippi, for allegedly disrespecting a white girl.[11]

King, and many others within Montgomery's black community, responded immediately to Rosa Parks's victimization. Outraged at her arrest, a black boycott of Montgomery's public bus system was quickly organized. At twenty-six years of age, King, the new minister in town, was elected president of the Montgomery Improvement Association, which was to guide the boycott. On December 2, 1955, the day after Rosa Parks refused to yield her bus seat, King stood before a packed church of protesters ready for action. The time had come to challenge the evils of segregation. And something inside King sensed this. He had no time to prepare a well-organized speech. He must speak on the spot, speak the word of God into an unpredictable and dangerous situation. The prophet, moved by God, spoke: "As you know, my friends, there comes a time when people get tired of being trampled over by the iron feet of oppression." The church erupted with applause and amens. King moved ahead presenting the prophet's logic, "If we are wrong—God Almighty is wrong! If we are wrong, Jesus of Nazareth was merely a utopian dreamer and never came down to Earth! If we are wrong, justice is a lie!"[12]

Writer Robert Ellsberg says, "It was an extraordinary speech that galvanized the struggle in Montgomery as surely as it launched King's career as a leader of the black freedom struggle in America."[13] It was as if God had prepared King all his life for this task. Out of his background and training, he was in the unique position of being able to speak to both white and black Americans. As a pastor from the black church tradition, he was able to mobilize forces from the strongest institution of African Americans. As an academic who had learned the ideals of American democracy and religion, he could challenge the political and moral conscience of mainstream America.

Over the next decade, beginning with the year-long bus boycott in Montgomery, King moved from crisis to crisis. He proclaimed and lived a philosophy of nonviolence and civil protest. His strategies were informed by Gandhi's experiences in India and grounded in his own understanding of the demands of the love ethic taught by Jesus. As leader of the Southern Christian Leadership Conference (SCLC), established in 1957, King focused his nation's attention on racism through sit-ins, freedom rides, voter registration, and boycotts. Thousands of protesters, black and white, placed their bodies on the line and were met by police harassment and the brutality of police dogs, fire hoses, and the clubs of law enforcement officers.

We cannot chronicle all of King's prophetic challenge to America here. What can be done, however, is to invite a reading, or rereading, of King's "Letter from Birmingham Jail." Much like the prophet Amos, King had to respond to the criticism of being an outsider, an agitator of unrest. White ministers in Birmingham, like the high priest Amaziah, accused King of moving too far, too fast—of asking too much. The Birmingham letter is King's reply. It is the reply of a prophet. Silence in the presence of injustice is not acceptable. King wrote:

> I am in Birmingham because injustice is here. Just as the eighth century prophets left their little villages and carried their "thus saith the Lord" far beyond the boundaries of their hometown; and just as the Apostle Paul left his little village of Tarsus . . . I too am compelled to carry the gospel of freedom beyond my particular hometown.[14]

So King persevered. Later in 1963, he stood at the Lincoln Memorial in Washington and declared his dream—a dream of an America in which his "four little children . . . will not be judged by the color of their skin but by the content of their character."[15]

The next year, 1964, the Civil Rights Bill was passed, and King received the prestigious Nobel Peace Prize. He was an international hero. But his land had not yet been healed. Injustice prevailed. Violence continued. It intruded into the SCLC marches from Selma to Montgomery. No longer able to remain silent about the violence of war, King spoke out against America's involvement in the war in Vietnam. Poverty in America was also abhorrent to King, and by the mid-1960s he had linked together the evils of racism, poverty, and militarism. The widening of King's prophetic concerns opened him to criticism from within his own ranks. Many within the civil rights movement began to worry that they were losing focus and support. But Martin the prophet persisted. Injustice was injustice wherever it was to be found.

Finally, the violence of the times consumed this great prophet of justice and peace. In Memphis to support striking sanitation workers, Martin Luther King Jr. was felled by a single shot from an assassin's rifle on the balcony of his motel headquarters. King had known for some time that his witness for love and justice might end with his early death. At age thirty-nine, a relatively young yet seasoned prophet of God was dead. But not his unfinished dream!

Love, Justice, and the Beloved Community

There have been others who have seen the prophetic connection between love and justice that Martin Luther King Jr. saw so clearly. However, few have articulated and demonstrated this relationship as effectively as King did. In fact, this may be a case of the twentieth-century prophet surpassing his prophetic teachers of ancient Israel. Eighth-century prophets like Amos acted out of love for God's covenant to declare the need for justice in the land. But their harsh judgments could and sometimes did lead to a pessimistic view of life. Even when they spoke of God's steadfast love (in Hebrew, *hesed*), as did the prophet Hosea, it was a hopeful view limited only to a faithful remnant.

King, by contrast, was optimistic to the core. This is not to say that his views were naively optimistic and shaped by impractical idealism. His optimism rather was grounded in his own suffering, his compassion for the cause, and his deep belief that God is in charge of the final, positive outcome of history. King understood that he was in the freedom struggle for the long run; and yet he knew he would probably not make it to that "promised land" of justice for all. But God would see it through to the final victory. Of this, King was sure. It was in this conviction that his eternal optimism rested.

King believed that God makes the love/justice connection even when we humans failed to do so. According to Coretta Scott King, her husband believed "in a divine, loving presence that binds all life." Furthermore, she said, "This belief was the force behind all of my husband's quests to eliminate social evil, and what he referred to when he preached of 'the interrelated structure of reality.'"[16] God made all the difference for King. He could not have carried on without this faith in God's compassion and justice.

King's life and witness cannot be understood without recognizing this most central fact of his existence: God is the God of love and justice. Nowhere is this made more clear than in his published book of sermons entitled, not coincidentally, *Strength to Love*. His sermon "A Tough Mind and a Tender Heart" cuts to the core of King's understanding of God's nature. According to King:

> The Bible, always clear in stressing both attributes of God, expresses his toughmindedness in his justice and wrath and his tenderheartedness in his love and grace. God has two outstretched arms. One is strong enough to surround us with justice, and one is gentle enough to embrace us with grace. On the one hand, God is a God of justice who punished Israel for her wayward deeds, and on the other hand, he is a forgiving father whose heart was filled with unutterable joy when the prodigal returned home.[17]

For King, we are embraced by the two outstretched arms of God, love and justice. But there is no coercion with God. Ultimately, acting in love and seeking justice is a cooperative endeavor between God and us. God and humanity are to work together.

In another sermon, "The Answer to a Perplexing Question," King elaborates on the theme of cooperation. "How," he asks, "can evil be cast out of our individual [the need for love] and collective [the need for justice] lives?" The answer lies not in relying completely upon God to do everything. We can't sit back and wait for divine intervention. Nor does the answer come only from human initiative and social engineering. "Rather," claims King, "both man and God, made one in a marvellous unity of purpose through an overflowing love as the free gift of himself on the part of God and by perfect obedience and receptivity on the part of man, can transform the old into the new and drive out the deadly cancer of sin."[18]

The new, transformed reality toward which King believed the human family was moving is the "beloved community." King's beloved community is to be the future realization of a world of peace and prosperity in which true justice is established for all. Within the civil rights movement itself, King thought he caught glimpses of this beloved community. People of different races, religions, and social realities worked together cooperatively for freedom through nonviolence with a sense of sacrifice for the greater good.

At the center of King's vision of the beloved community is a commitment to acts of love that also create the possibility for justice. King believed the social forces of love are only beginning to be discovered, even though the prophets hinted at it and Jesus uncovered it in his Sermon on the Mount. The truth is that we still have a long way to go. According to King, it wasn't until the twentieth century that Mahatma Gandhi made the first serious effort to translate Jesus' teachings into a massive strategy for social change. Gandhi's program of active, nonviolent resistance to injustice was only a start at the social application of Jesus' gospel of love on a grand scale. More is to come.

King affirmed throughout his life that the moral imperative to love is the only force capable of eradicating socially entrenched injustices like racism, poverty, and war. All else will fail in the long run, but not love. Love as a moral force is yet to be given its full opportunity for success. Within a year of his death, King made perhaps his most eloquent statement about love. Addressing the anti-war group Clergy and Laity Concerned, he professed:

> When I speak of love, I am not speaking of some sentimental and weak response. I am speaking of that force which all of the great religions have seen as the unifying principle of life. Love is somehow the key that unlocks the door which leads to ultimate reality. This Hindu-Moslem-Christian-Jewish-Buddhist belief about ultimate reality is beautifully summed up in the first epistle of Saint John: "Let us love one another; for love is of God and everyone that loveth is born of God and knoweth God."[19]

This notion of love, in King's estimate, leads directly to the difficult path of justice. He knew this kind of love would mean personal suffering for himself and many others in the movement. He faced this issue early and often as he moved in his journey from Montgomery to Memphis. Early on, King admitted to a time of doubt during the Montgomery bus boycott. Day after day, he had received numerous threatening phone calls and hate mail.

Finally, the breaking point was reached. A phone caller late one night made an especially ugly threat: "Listen, nigger, we've taken all we want from you. Before next week you'll be sorry you ever came to Montgomery." King reports that he hung up the phone, and unable to sleep, sat in his kitchen with a pot of coffee heating. He confesses, "I was ready to give up."[20]

Then, as he sat with a cup of coffee, he bowed his head and prayed aloud for help. In response to his prayer, King said, "I could hear the quiet assurance of an inner voice saying, 'Stand up for righteousness, stand up for truth, God will be at your side forever.'" In that moment, King's fears passed. His uncertainties disappeared: "I was ready to face anything. The outer situation remained the same, but God had given me inner calm."[21]

Three nights later, Martin Luther King Jr.'s house was bombed. And so it is for a prophet. I'm convinced that God places prophets before us as signs, as witnesses to love and justice. They seek to open our eyes to those things that are most precious to God. Dare we look? Dare we examine our own hearts and minds in relation to the prophet's message. Dare we be different? Dare we be divinely discontented and hopelessly maladjusted? God would have it so, for the sake of love and justice.

CHAPTER TWELVE

Something Beautiful for God

"'Come, you that are blessed by my Father, inherit the kingdom prepared for you from the foundation of the world; for I was hungry and you gave me food, I was thirsty and you gave me something to drink, I was a stranger and you welcomed me, I was naked and you gave me clothing, I was sick and you took care of me, I was in prison and you visited me.' Then the righteous will answer him, 'Lord, when was it that we saw you hungry and gave you food, or thirsty and gave you something to drink? And when was it that we saw you a stranger and welcomed you, or naked and gave you clothing? And when was it that we saw you sick or in prison and visited you?' And the king will answer them, 'Truly I tell you, just as you did it to one of the least of these who are members of my family, you did it to me.'"

MATTHEW 25:34–40

If you want to do something beautiful for God, look at your own family and the poor around you.

It is a gift from God for you to be able to serve him in your families and in his poor. Even if it is one person only, that one is still your brother or sister.

Nationality doesn't matter.

Color doesn't matter.

Being rich or poor doesn't matter.

That person is your brother or your sister.

And how do we know this? Because Jesus said, "Whatever you do for the least of my brothers, you do it to me."

MOTHER TERESA, *Loving Jesus*

WHY DO WE OFTEN READ THE BIBLE so selectively, taking what confirms our beliefs and prejudices as literal truth and leaving the rest open for abstract interpretations? The twenty-fifth chapter of Matthew's Gospel presents us with a direct literal challenge. We are told to care for the needs of the hungry, the thirsty, the stranger, the naked, the sick, and the prisoner. We are to do this because in the suffering of others we meet Christ himself. The suffering and Jesus Christ cannot be separated; to love one is to love the other. What could be clearer and more compelling? And yet we sometimes try to explain this passage away.

The Gospel of Matthew does not let us off the hook on this most central teaching of Christian discipleship. As we shall discover, neither did Mother Teresa of Calcutta. In studying Matthew's Gospel, we find that its entire narrative leads to this one unmistakable conclusion. Mother Teresa also repeated the theme of loving Jesus by serving others. In fact, this was the spiritual basis for all she did. Matthew 25 was quoted more often by Mother Teresa than any other Bible passage.

What more could be said? The Bible's teaching on love boils down to this: What we do to the least of these our brothers and sisters, we do to Jesus. There is no escape, no exit, from this greatest of all divine mandates. Matthew knew it. Mother Teresa knew it. And somewhere deep within our hearts, we know it too! But as we shall discover, what our heart knows to be true isn't always acted upon. That is the tragedy of Matthew 25.

God through Christ presents each of us with a wonderful opportunity to do "something beautiful for God."[1] So say Matthew 25 and Mother Teresa. In Christ, our love for others, especially those in need, is a pleasure rather than an obligation or a religious requirement. Love simply loves. This is what Matthew's Gospel and Mother Teresa are telling us in so many different ways. But always, there is only one essential truth—love of God and neighbor is one and the same.

The Teaching Gospel

The Gospel according to Matthew has rightfully been called the church's teacher. It proclaims Jesus' life, death, and resurrection and is oriented toward defining discipleship for Christians of every age. And at the heart of that definition is an invitation to compassion, to love God, neighbors, and one's self. Passages in Matthew, like the Sermon on the Mount (Matthew 5–7), emphasize this kind of compassionate discipleship that Jesus is advocating.

We are told in Matthew 5 that Jesus ascended a mountain in order to teach. This should alert us as the reader of the Gospel to pay close attention for what comes next. After all, Moses brought the commandments of God down from a mountain! Jesus' Sermon on the Mount begins with the Beatitudes (Matthew 5:3–11), which present a most astounding reversal of the world's values. Those who mourn and are meek (without power in this world) are to be blessed by God—not those who are triumphant and have worldly success, those who seem to have a charmed life. Also to be blessed are those who hunger and search for righteousness (justice and truth), not those who already have all the answers and who are willing to answer other people's questions as well.

Perhaps the most blessed of God are those who show mercy, not those who seek to get even. Jesus, in the Sermon on the Mount, celebrates those who live in simplicity with a pure heart. Those who pursue peace and suffer persecution for God's kingdom are likewise declared blessed. Soon a picture begins to emerge. Jesus' disciples are to be compassionate souls who love life by loving others. Indeed, in the remainder of the sermon, we learn about the character of a true disciple. He or she is to be slow to anger, faithful in relationships, honest and non-judgmental, a lover of others, even enemies, and uncomplicated in devotion to God: simple prayers, private fasting, uncluttered joy (Matthew 5:21–6:34). The so-called Golden Rule places a capstone upon these teachings. "In everything do to others as you would have them do to you; for this [says Jesus] is the law and the prophets" (Matthew 7:12).

The teachings about discipleship in the Sermon on the Mount represent one of five lengthy discourses by Jesus in Matthew's Gospel. Many scholars believe that the writer of Matthew arranged Jesus' teachings in five clusters in order to suggest a parallel with the five discourses of Moses found in the book of Deuteronomy. Thus, Jesus' teachings in the New Testament are matched with Moses' teachings in the Old Testament. Jesus' five sets of teachings in Matthew include the Sermon on the Mount, the missionary discourse, a collection of parables, a community discourse, and the final judgment discourse.[2] Shortly, our focus will be upon the fifth and final of these teachings of Jesus—the last-judgment discourse.

Matthew's Gospel has more of Jesus' teachings than do any of the other New Testament Gospels. This may explain why early Christianity placed Matthew's Gospel first in its arrangement of New Testament writings. Most scholars, as was noted in chapter 9, identify Mark as the earliest written of the New Testament Gospels. If historical sequence were the issue, Mark's Gospel would be first in the New Testament's ordering. But later generations rightfully placed Matthew's teaching Gospel first. The church was anxious to instruct its membership. It is quite probable that the author of the Gospel of Matthew was a teacher within the early church writing in the last quarter of the first century. In a sense, he stood in the tradition of the rabbis, or teachers, of Judaism.

According to tradition, the author of this teaching Gospel is said to be Matthew the tax collector, one of the original twelve disciples. But few scholars believe this to be so. Authorship, detectable from the content of the Gospel itself, as Raymond Brown argues, is most likely identified with an unknown Jewish Christian teacher from the last quarter of the first century who lived outside of Palestine in the Antioch region.[3] We can tell from the Gospel's composition that this writer was Greek-speaking, that he probably knew Aramaic and Hebrew, and that he drew upon the Gospel of Mark for help in constructing his Gospel. Other oral and written sources were also consulted, including other collections of Jesus' sayings. The Q source postulated by scholars would be an example of other written or oral sources that probably inspired the writer of Matthew's Gospel. Finally, there was probably a teaching tradition bearing Matthew's name that associated itself with Jesus' disciple of the same name.

Whoever wrote the Gospel of Matthew, it is clear that its author wanted those who read his work to recognize that Jesus the Messiah was a teaching Messiah. Thus, we have in this New Testament witness not only a teaching Gospel but also a teaching Jesus. The writer of Matthew's Gospel carefully builds the lines of Jesus' teaching from discourse to discourse, until we reach the twenty-fifth chapter. Here we find the climatic point of Jesus' teaching ministry. The Gospel writer has guided us through five long discourses of Jesus' instructions until we find ourselves at the story of the last judgment. Near the end of the Gospel, it stands as a touring affirmation of discipleship, a call to live a life of compassion.

Encouragement to Love

Scholar Eugene Boring notes that Matthew 25:31–46 has the clear intent of encouragement.[4] These final words of Jesus' last discourse are set off in the context of the apocalyptic, that is, they speak of what is to be disclosed at the end times. Here is the last word on things! Following a long series of six parables and encouragements to live responsibly, the Gospel narrative introduces a story about the coming of the Son of Man. Jesus has already identified himself with the Son of Man, who is to come at the end of the age, and so the early Christian readers will understand this to be Jesus' reference to his return in glory at the conclusion of history.

Jesus, as the returning Son of Man, will be a judge. A final judgment will be rendered. But there is an unexpected surprise for ancient and modern readers. The criterion for this final reckoning is not a confession of faith in Jesus Christ, as many Christians would expect. Nor is it adherence to religious law or the worship of God. According to Boring, "Nothing is said of grace, justification, or the forgiveness of sins." Rather, the only thing that matters is whether or not Jesus' followers have acted compassionately toward those in need—with loving care. To quote Boring again, "Such deeds are not a matter of 'extra credit,' but constitute the decisive criterion of judgment."[5]

How unusual! In the only scene from the New Testament in which we have a description of the last judgment, our picture is that of the separation of sheep from goats. Interestingly, in this imagery the sheep and the goats do not stand for true and false believers to be separated between heaven and hell. Nor in our modern parlance could they be said to be Christians and Muslims, or Democrats and Republicans, or liberals and fundamentalists, and so forth. There is no religious or cultural or political litmus test. We are not to be judged by our theology and ideologies.

The only thing that counts is love. Compassion is the sole criterion for the judgment that people bring upon themselves in the last judgment story. In Matthew's Gospel, Jesus had taught throughout, says Boring, that "self-giving care for others is the heart of the revealed will of God in the Torah."[6] In accord with the teachings of the law and the prophets, Jesus made love the measure (Matthew 5:17–48; 7:12; 22:34–40) of all human intentions and actions. To take care of one another, especially those in need, is the only thing that matters in the end. To serve (in Greek, *diakoneo*) others in the name of God is the only form of true discipleship (Matthew 25:44).

The judgment story in Matthew 25 is clearly not a parable. It differs significantly from the parable style used elsewhere by Jesus in Matthew. Parables, as we have learned, begin with the familiar, with an everyday setting. They then often move through a series of twists and surprising turns to describe a new dimension of life, an alternative reality. However, apocalyptic stories, like the last judgment account, work in reverse fashion. They begin with the unfamiliar, an otherworldly depiction of end things. This is not a scene from daily life. The Son of Man has returned in glory, with a host of angels, and sits on the throne in glory. This spectacular scene continues as the nations (peoples) of the world gather before him, and he separates people as a shepherd would separate sheep from goats. This simile is used to depict the final judgment. All this, of course, is far from the realm of everyday experience.

But suddenly, this extraordinary story returns to the ordinary—to the mundane, to the arena of recognizable acts of human compassion. Down from the heights of apocalyptic drama, we find ourselves confronted with basic human needs. Several examples are given. Those who are hungry, thirsty, and without clothing are mentioned. Also, the sick, the stranger, and the prisoner are presented before the nations. We have seen these people before in Matthew's Gospel. They are among the blessed ones of the Beatitudes.

In Matthew 25, Jesus as the King, sitting in judgment, identifies directly with those who suffer. "Truly I tell you, just as you did it to one of the least of those who are members of my family, you did it to me" (Matthew 25:40). All those who suffer, then, are Jesus' brothers and sisters—and our brothers and sisters! As the story continues, those at the king's right hand (the sheep) are told to come into a kingdom that has been prepared for them. They do so because they have responded to the needs of others. Indeed, they are so selfless in their actions that they are unaware that they are in fact responding to the king, Christ. As far as they know, they are simply responding to basic human need.

However, those at the king's left hand (the goats) are accursed and sent into "the eternal fire." This judgment is based not upon their theology but upon their ethics. They have failed to respond to fellow human beings who are suffering and in need. And by failing to do this, they have failed to respond to God in their midst—Immanuel, "God with us." Jesus is to be found in all those who suffer.

Jesus as the messianic king makes it clear that the message of God's kingdom—or the reign of God—consists primarily of compassion (Matthew 25:40). Love for others is the key to discipleship, and it follows the path of service set forth by Jesus himself. Love is our most faithful response to God's kingdom having drawn near. There is no substitute for this spirituality of compassion. Right views cannot be a substitute for right action. To be right is not the same as to do right. In our theology, we know who God is by what God does, and in our spirituality we know who we are by what we do. Matthew 25 reminds us that to know and love God through Jesus Christ is to live compassionately.

The Common Glory

The central teaching of the Gospel of Matthew (and the other Gospels) calls us to a common glory. This common glory is love. We need not be brilliant theologians to discover the depths of this most crucial of all of Jesus' teachings. And Matthew's Gospel is careful to ensure that we don't miss this simple truth. As in Mark and Luke, the Great Commandment of Jesus dominates the landscape of Matthew's Gospel (Matthew 22:37–38). In the midst of conflict, Jesus reminds his disciples and his adversaries about what must never be forgotten. Remember to love! Remember the *Shema* of ancient tradition! Remember love.

The *Shema* (Deuteronomy 6:4–5) began with an affirmation of the oneness of God and then teaches that we are to love God with our entire being.

> Hear, O Israel: The LORD is our God, the Lord alone. You shall love the Lord your God with all your heart, and with all your soul, and with all your might.

In Matthew 28:34–35, Jesus repeats this call to love God. According to Eugene Boring, the *Shema* is "the closest thing to a universal creed in Judaism."[7] Jesus then adds to this a call to love the neighbor (Leviticus 19:18). This second commandment to love one's neighbor had already been expanded by Jesus in the Sermon on the Mount to include our enemies as well as our friends.

Thus, just before the fifth and last of the teaching discourses, Matthew's Gospel once again reinforces Jesus' emphasis on love. In this one Great Commandment in Matthew 22, Jesus masterfully summarizes the 613 commandments of the Torah, the teachings of ancient Israel. By Jesus' day, the rabbis of his faith had counted 613 commands (248 positive commands, corresponding to the number of parts of the body, and 365 negative commands, corresponding to the days of the year). Fortunately for us, Jesus cut through to the core of these ancient teachings, to the heart and soul of God's commandments—the law of love. In a sense, he told people what they already knew: love is to be the heart of any genuine response to God.

The word for love, *agape,* used by the writer of Matthew is the Greek term often used in the New Testament for compassion. *Agape* is what Jesus taught and demonstrated through his own actions. But there is nothing magic about this Greek word. As Boring cautions, Jesus' understanding of love mentioned here and elsewhere in the New Testament "is not bound up with the meaning of a particular Greek word."[8] *Agape* has no inherent meaning that refers only to the love of God and neighbor. For example, in 2 Peter 2:15, *agape* is used for Balaam's love of money, and in Luke 6:32 it is used for sinners' love for each other. In John 3:19, it is used for the love of evil people for darkness.

However, Jesus' followers gave new meaning to the word. When the first Christians used *agape,* they were referring to their new experience of God in Jesus. It included compassion for others and a radical form of life-giving sacrifice. In essence, the word *agape* had been transformed, just as the lives of those who followed Jesus had been transformed. There was a common glory among Jesus' followers, and by any name or word, it was a commitment to life-changing compassion.

Compassion is the true common glory of Christianity. But so often this has been forgotten. And compassion has been replaced by dogma, doctrine, and church loyalty. Yet, should we take Jesus' story of the last judgment seriously, our common glory is not orthodoxy, or right praise, but orthopraxis, or right practice. Only in loving can the follower of Jesus also truly worship. The words of the folk hymn say it best: "And they'll know we are Christians by our love, by our love, Yes, they'll know we are Christians by our love."[9]

Mother Teresa (1910–1997)

The greatest legacy of Mother Teresa is her conviction that each of us is capable of love. The expression "We all can't be Mother Teresa" has made its way into our common vocabulary. In a sense however, this undercuts what Mother Teresa attempted to teach. Not that she would want us all to be Mother Teresas. But she would want us to know that each of us can do something beautiful for God. We can love another human being.

Accordingly, Mother Teresa often quoted from Matthew 25 and its story of the sheep and the goats. In light of this passage, she believed that we must be prepared to love every moment of every day of our lives. Her teaching is the same as that of Jesus, the king in Matthew's judgment narrative, "Truly I tell you, just as you did it to one of the least of these . . . you did it to me" (Matthew 25:40). The reverse is also true for Mother Teresa. "Truly I tell you, just as you did not do it to one of the least of these, you did not do it to me" (Matthew 25:45). Mother Teresa doesn't want us to miss the opportunities to love that God places before us.

Love in action was the ultimate expression of faith for Mother Teresa. Similarly, failure to love is a blatant rejection of God and Jesus. There was no middle ground for this saintly woman. Either one loves God and loves neighbor, or else all efforts at spirituality and ethics are a waste of time. Likewise, for Mother Teresa, a secure foundation for a compassionate life can be found only in God. All other foundations are without spiritual substance and will fail us in the end.

A mere reading of Mother Teresa's words and what others have to say about her, both positive and negative, can never provide an adequate picture of her life and contributions to humanity. We can gain a proper perspective on Mother Teresa only by assessing her by her own criterion—love in action. What is to be learned from a person many considered a modern saint? How can Mother Teresa shed further light on our *lectio divina* of Matthew 25? Who is the woman behind the legend of the saint?

Behind the Legend

The one whom the world knows as Mother Teresa of Calcutta was born to Nicholas Bojaxhin and Dranafile Bernai Bojaxhin on August 26, 1910, in Skopje, Yugoslavia. She was christened Agnes and called Gonxha (flower bud) within her Albanian family. Her hometown was in the kingdom of Albania, which had been a part of the Ottoman Empire until the political formation of Yugoslavia. She grew up within a small Catholic minority in a geographic region that was largely Muslim.[10]

Agnes Bojaxhin's home life was happy and secure in the beginning. In addition to her loving parents, there was a brother and a sister. Her religious instruction at home was casual and informal, although Mother Teresa has emphasized that her mother "taught us to love God and to love our neighbour."[11] Life changed dramatically, however, in 1917 when Agnes's father met an untimely death. According to Anne Sebba's biography, the death of Agnes's father by poisoning had resulted from Nicholas Bojaxhin's political efforts to gain national rights for Albanians in Yugoslavia. The situation in the Balkans in the early twentieth century was as complex and unsettled as it is today, maybe even more so, if that is possible.

Agnes's family survived their tragic loss with determination and resolve. Her mother started a small business selling embroidered cloth in order to keep her family together. The family's perseverance in the face of tragedy, according to biographer Navin Chawla, made a deep impression on little Agnes. During this time of crisis, the family drew closer to the Church of the Sacred Heart in Skopje. This helped to reinforce their cultural and religious identity.

Mother Teresa has been reluctant to speak of her childhood. When interviewed, she has preferred to place the focus upon her missionary work and not her family origins. But she has indicated that her family provided a solid grounding, especially spiritually. She remembers her family, led by her mother and father, praying together each evening. Along these lines, Mother Teresa also recalls her initial interest in a religious vocation: "I was twelve years old . . . when I first felt the desire to become a nun."[12] This may have resulted from her family's open acceptance of anyone who was in need. Although her family was poor, Agnes remembers additional "relatives" regularly sharing meals at the Bojaxhin kitchen table. Later, Agnes realized that the extra guests at mealtime were not relatives but often strangers.

Mother Teresa has a keen memory of her mother washing and covering the sores of an alcoholic woman. She also remembers her mother visiting a mother of six in her dying days. This kind of compassion for those who suffered must have greatly contributed to Agnes's own spiritual formation and future ambitions. As a teenager, Agnes helped to give religious instruction to children. More and more she began to view herself as a religious teacher. Finally, at the age of eighteen, a remarkably mature Agnes decided to leave home and become a teaching missionary with the Sisters of Loreto order in Bengal. She left home on September 26, 1928, never to see her mother again. First she traveled to Ireland for training with the Loreto religious order, and then on to her beloved India, where she would live and serve the remainder of her life.

After nearly two decades as a Sister of Loreto, Sister Teresa, as Agnes Bojaxhin was now known, received a second calling, or as she has said, "a call within a call."[13] Traveling on a train to Darjeeling, a hill station in the Himalayas, Sister Teresa had arrived at the conviction she had a new calling within her ministry. Even though she had been a successful teacher in her order's school in India, something seemed to be missing. She had been thinking about working directly with the poor. Now she was certain. God had confirmed her interests. "He wanted me to be poor with the poor and to love him in the distressing disguise of the poorest of the poor."[14]

I am in awe of people who make dramatic, positive changes at midlife. At a time when most of us are finally settling on a vocation, some risk everything—not for personal gain but out of a desire to follow a new leading from God. In this instance, it was a highly respected, teaching nun setting off in a new direction. In our *lectio divina,* we have seen this before—St. Augustine, Martin Luther, John Wesley, Desmond Tutu, and Madeleine L'Engle. All these individuals were well into their thirties when they heard God's calling, yet again. Perhaps we had better keep our ears open. God, it seems, may not be done with us. We each continue to be a marvelous work in progress. And God continues to call. We'd better listen.

In Sister Teresa's case God certainly wasn't done—and had only just begun. She gained permission from her order to leave the convent. What happened next is history. In Robert Ellsberg's words:

In place of her traditional religious habit she donned a simple white sari with blue border and went out to seek Jesus in the desperate byways of Calcutta. Eventually she was joined by others—including many of her former students. They became the Missionaries of Charity. And she became Mother Teresa.[15]

However, for many years, Mother Teresa and her new religious order worked in obscurity in the slums of Calcutta. They sought to help the poorest of the poor in Jesus' name. They ministered to the sick, the homeless, the unwanted—especially orphans. Eventually Mother Teresa's work came to be identified with her home for the dying in Calcutta. In the Home for the Dying (Kalighat), destitute and dying men and women were gathered from the streets and given loving care and respect in their last days. It was said by a growing number of admirers that those who had lived like "animals in the gutter" were enabled to "die like angels" among the Sisters of Charity.[16]

Mother Teresa was eventually discovered by the world at large. Several documentary films were made of the work of the Missionaries of Charity. Also, Mother Teresa permitted a few interviews related to her work, and small books of her speeches and sayings were published. In 1979 Mother Teresa was awarded the Nobel Peace Prize. Some began to speak of this small woman as a living saint. Mother Teresa, however, tried to point the attention back to the work of her order. In one of her best-known quotes, Mother Teresa reminded her admirers—and anyone else who would listen—that "We can do no great things, only small things with great love." Focus was to be upon acts of compassion and not upon the actors. We can all do small things with great love, according to this saintly woman. God doesn't need heroes; God needs coworkers doing small acts of compassion without fanfare. This is what truly changes the world from Mother Teresa's perspective. Jesus would agree.

Distressing Disguises

Mother Teresa has taught that Christ comes to us in many different disguises. In speaking of her Missionaries of Charity, she has said:

> We are taught from the very first moment to discover Christ under the distressing disguise of the poor, the sick, the outcasts. Christ presents himself to us under every disguise: the dying, the paralytic, the leper, the invalid, the orphan. It is faith that makes our work, which demands both special preparation and a special calling, easy or at least more bearable.[17]

The Missionaries of Charity indeed work under very difficult circumstances. Yet, no matter what the physical or mental condition of those they serve, no matter how physically repulsive the disease is, Christ is seen as present in each person who is in need. The afflicted and dying are treated with the utmost respect by the Missionaries of Charity. Every individual is seen as being made in the image of God, and therefore each is of infinite worth and value. Christ himself, the very embodiment of God, is to be discovered in every person served.

Navin Chawla reports that while writing Mother Teresa's official biography he discovered a hand-drawn chart on a parlor wall at the Missionaries of Charity headquarters, an old-three story building in Calcutta. It lists specifically how Christ would be met that particular day in the order's houses of charity in more than one hundred different countries. According to Chawla, "The social activities included child welfare and educational schemes, family visiting, day crèches, feeding programs and homes of alcoholics, night shelters and natural family planning centres." Also listed were medical activities such as "dispensaries, leprosy clinics and rehabilitation centres, homes for the abandoned, crippled and mentally retarded children, for unwed mothers, for sick and dying destitutes and AIDS patients."[18] In addition, the list recorded educational activities involving various schools, and sewing and commercial and handicraft classes. Finally, the listing included "prison visiting, family contacts, catechism classes, Catholic action groups and Sunday Schools."[19] In all these examples, Christ was present in the thousands of people being met and helped.

All this began with one woman, Mother Teresa, alone in Calcutta, with a call within a call to serve the poorest of the poor. It took a long time for her to gain the approval of the Sisters of Loreto and the Vatican for her new venture. Her request was out of the ordinary. She was asking for permission to work on her own directly with the poor as a vowed nun. Nuns did not usually do such things in this manner. But God was not to be denied, and neither was the one who had begun her life as Agnes Bojaxhin. Mother Teresa would leave her convent and live among the poor—in poverty without a demand upon any others for her financial support.

The Sisters of Loreto eventually were very helpful and supportive. But Mother Teresa insisted upon being a mendicant, begging for her own food, while working with the poor. In India, mendicancy had been an ancient and honored way of life among holy men and teachers. Thus when Mother Teresa went begging for support of her first projects—a school for the poor and a dispensary—she was to serve within an honored Indian tradition, albeit quite unusual for a Catholic nun. Almost everything Mother Teresa did in the late 1940s and early 1950s was out of the ordinary. Yet all she did was dedicated to the common glory of God's love. Most unusual, perhaps, was the establishment of the Home for Dying Destitute opened in August 1952. By this time Mother Teresa was no longer working alone. There were now nearly thirty women in her growing Order of the Missionaries of Charity, authorized by Rome in 1950.

The Home for the Dying Destitute is a story in itself. Mother Teresa had managed to acquire a home for the destitute at Kalighat, an old Hindu temple in the heart of Calcutta. The great majority of those who came to the home were Hindu. And they still are. According to Navin Chawla, "Only devout Hindus or the most intrepid tourists make their way to Kalighat."[19] Kalighat, in one of the most congested areas of the city, is not easy to locate. The name given this site by the Sisters of Charity is Nirmal Hriday (in Bengali, House of the Sacred Heart), which, although a Catholic term, is acceptable to Hindus.

Chawla's description of Nirmal Hriday is worthy of a lengthy quote because it captures so beautifully the spiritual essence of this work. It has been called "Mother's first love."

> I entered a hall crammed with low stretcher beds, placed row upon row on an antiseptic, scrubbed floor. To my right, there was the reception area with some work tables, and nearby there were a couple of patients on stretchers. These, I discovered later, were the very sick on whom the Sisters might keep a special eye as they went about their ministering. There must have been a hundred emaciated bodies, each lying in a bed with a number printed on the wall behind it. . . . There was hardly a sound above the rustle of the saris or the ministering of some treatment, in contrast to the noisy and polluted street, a few feet away.[20]

Because the work of the Missionaries of Charity is a Christian mission, criticisms have been leveled against the order for being more interested in saving souls than relieving suffering. But for Mother Teresa, there was no need for converting souls, for baptisms, and for deathbed conversions. Chawla says that in living with Christ and in serving him through the poor, Mother Teresa witnessed to her faith. The remainder, she said, was up to God.

When Chawla put the question of conversion directly to Mother Teresa, she answered with a gleeful twist of irony. "I do convert," she said, "I convert you to be a better Hindu, a better Catholic, a better Muslim, or Jain or Buddhist. I want to help you to find God. When you find him, it is up to you to do what you want with him."[21] The witness was Mother Teresa's, but the relationship is between the individual and

God. When we stop to think about it, what more can be said? Further pronouncements, as if to speak for God, and to know the mind of God, are presumptuous. We cannot speak for God. Not even Mother Teresa could do that. We can only witness to God's love.

What about Saints?

By all accounts, those who knew Mother Teresa in her early years with the Sisters of Loreto did not find her to be an exceptional person. She was considered a good nun who worked hard and had a deep devotion to God. This could be said of many others in her religious order. So what made Mother Teresa—Mother Teresa?

What made Mother Teresa different was the special work to which she dedicated her life. Many came to view this diminutive Albanian nun, an adopted daughter of India, as the personification of Christ-like love. In humility, she accepted this role with grace and dignity. She did not aspire to sainthood. She did all she did for the glory of God and the work of the Missionaries of Charity. By 1990, 456 centers had been founded in more than 100 countries, with about 4,000 members of the order feeding 500,000 families, serving 20,000 slum children, ministering to 90,000 leprosy patients, caring for 17,000 shut-ins, and running six AIDS shelters. And the list goes on.[22]

Mother Teresa was not without her critics. Close to the end of her life, mounting criticisms were leveled against the one whom many hailed a living saint. Some of the criticism has been without foundation and infinitely unfair. Often Mother Teresa was criticized not for what she had done but for what she hadn't done. For example, she has been criticized for not addressing the root causes of poverty and suffering, although her order has extended kindness and care to millions. The Missionaries of Charity were never designed as a movement for social activism. Their charge has always been direct care for the suffering.

More realistic criticisms of Mother Teresa have come from Anne Sebba, a London-based writer. Her book on Mother Teresa raises important questions. Although respectful of Mother Teresa's early achievements, Sebba wonders if time had not passed her by. Was her theology too simplistic and reactionary; were her medical practices too dated and uniformed; was she too close to world leaders, especially dictators; and were her views on abortion and birth control wildly unrealistic?[23]

Certainly this is not the place to answer Mother Teresa's critics. Neither the criticisms nor responses to the criticisms can be given adequate space here. But the criticisms do remind us that Mother Teresa was as human as she was saintly. And this is her common glory to be shared with the rest of us. None of us are above reproach or criticism, not even Mother Teresa. We are all still moving on to the perfection of love that God has given us.

No amount of criticism, however, can diminish the just and honorable work of Mother Teresa. She set out to do something beautiful for God, and she did. Like Mother Teresa, we are called to do something beautiful for God, to see Christ in others. That is what Matthew 25 asks of us. That is what Mother Teresa asks of us. How are we prepared to minister to those in the distressing disguises of Christ? No other question mattered to Mother Teresa.

One of the greatest tributes paid to Mother Teresa was an award from a group called Bharatiys Vedya Bhavan, a respected Indian organization created for the regeneration of Indian culture and values. When Mother Teresa was given this organization's highest honor, it was stated that she was "a quiet but courageous crusader who, in a God-inspired moment, launched a mission of mercy and compassion, reaching out to alleviate the suffering of millions the world over—the nameless, voiceless, homeless, depressed and dispossessed." The citation ends with these perceptive words, "She is one of those rare souls who has transcended all barriers of race, religion, creed and nation. She aspires for no kingdom, no honour, not even salvation or *moksha*. She is a true *Vaishnavayana*—minstrel of God—wholly dedicated to the removal of *peeda paraayi* (the pain of others), in the manner of Mahatma Gandhi."[24]

Mother Teresa had become a part of the soul of India. She had become a part of the entire world—all because she sought to fulfill the mandate for love in Matthew 25. She also has become a part of each of us. Whenever and wherever we are opened to the reality of Christ, the Lord of distressing disguises, we are reminded of Mother Teresa's commitment. "Truly, I tell you, just as you do it to one of the least of these . . . you did it to me" (Matthew 25:40).

AFTERWORD
Enter to Pray, Leave to Serve

I WAS RECENTLY STRUCK by a simple heading placed in a congregation's printed order of worship. It read, "Enter to pray, leave to serve." That is what our silent conversations with the Bible have been all about. My hope is that in our reflections on the Bible and the saints and sages of Christianity, you the reader have met the living God and been blessed. Furthermore, I hope that we have entered this *lectio divina* with prayerful expectation and as a result are prepared to leave to serve.

The most important thing in our study has been what has happened to our hearts and minds as we have read and meditated upon these pages. If some of the readings have left you cold, then it should be attributed to my shortcomings as a writer. When your spirits have soared and been lifted toward God, then it is all to the glory and working of the Holy Spirit. This writing project has been for the spiritual enlightenment of the reader. My hunch is that God has opened us to insights that neither you nor I could have anticipated. This is the way the Word of God works in our lives. We have little control over where and when the Spirit moves us.

Thus these reflections have been a starting point—and only a starting point—for our continued spiritual encounter. There are so many more rich passages of Scripture that can be mined for their hidden treasures. We have only scratched the surface, but it is a start. Likewise, the cloud of witnesses is so numerous in Christian tradition that I have been able to call out only the names of those who have especially influenced my life. I have been so bold as to assume that these particular men and women of faith might have a special word for our day. If time and space had permitted, I would have explored more of the writings of the Old Testament prophets and more of Jesus' parables, not to mention the book of Hebrews. And the list goes on.

There are many other men and women of faith whose lives and words open the Bible for me. I would add to my own list Origen, Anselm, Abelard, Francis of Assisi, Hildegard of Bingen, Catherine of Sienna, John Calvin, Jonathan Edwards, Sojourner Truth, Elizabeth Cady Stanton, Walter Rauschenbusch, Georgia Harkness, Dorothy Day, Oscar Romero, Jitsuo Morikawa, Dom Helder Camara, and Pope John XXIII.

It is a truism that God never leaves us without witnesses. And through these witnesses, God's grace abides with us still, to use Luther's words. When our hearts and minds are quieted, we are able to catch wonderful glimpses of God. That's what this book has been about. If the spirit within us is truly willing, we will meet the living God. As the heading on the church bulletin suggests, we enter to pray—to encounter the Divine. Having done so, we now leave to serve in God's holy name with Christ as our guide. Do we understand everything? No. Will we ever? Probably not. But might we have faith and hope, and be perfected in love? The Word of God answers with a resounding yes!

According to the hymn writer Charles Wesley, nothing can keep us from serving God if that is our heart's true desire. And by so doing, we too will find ourselves "lost in wonder, love, and praise." Oh, to lose our lives in God—to find a more faithful, hopeful, and loving way. That is our true goal and end in life.

Prayer: *O gracious God, help each of us to truly lose ourselves in your wonder, love, and praise. Then all conversations will finally cease, for we will know one another face to face beyond all words. And in silence, we will be at home in you. Amen.*

NOTES

PREFACE

1. All quotes from the Bible in this book are from the New Revised Standard Version unless otherwise indicated. Psalm 145:3 in the preface is from the King James Version because it is consistent with John K. Ryan's translation of Augustine's *Confessions.*
2. This type of spiritual reading, which was popularized by St. Benedict (c. 480–c. 547), requires a thoughtful mind and a patient heart in the exploration of Holy Scripture.

CHAPTER ONE

1. Thomas Merton, *The Seven Storey Mountain* (New York: Harcourt Brace Jovanovich, 1948), 208.
2. Thomas Merton, *Seeds of Contemplation* (New York: Dell, 1949), 11.
3. Thomas Merton, *The Sign of Jonas* (Garden City, N.Y.: Image Books, 1956), 21.
4. Merton, *The Seven Storey Mountain,* 410.
5. Merton, *The Sign of Jonas,* 235.
6. Ibid., 212.
7. Thomas Merton, *Opening the Bible* (Collegeville, Minn.: The Liturgical Press, 1970), 34–35. Merton's unpublished notes for *Opening the Bible* reveal a heavy use of Karl Barth, *Word of God, Word of Man* (New York: Harper & Row Publishers, 1957), 51–96.
8. Merton, *The Sign of Jonas,* 212.
9. Ibid., 220.
10. Thomas Merton, *Conjectures of a Guilty Bystander* (Garden City, N.Y.: Doubleday, 1966), 156.
11. Ibid., 157.

CHAPTER TWO

1. Russell Pregeant, *Engaging the New Testament* (Minneapolis: Fortress, 1995), 111; quoting Dan Otto Via Jr., *The Parables: Their Literary and Existential Dimension* (Philadelphia: Fortress, 1967), 171.
2. Robert W. Funk, *Honest to Jesus* (San Francisco: HarperSanFrancisco, 1996), 167.

3. John Dominic Crossan, *The Dark Interval* (Niles, Ill.: Argus Communications, 1975), 123.

4. Dom Helder Camara, *A Thousand Reasons for Living* (Philadelphia: Fortress, 1981), 71.

5. Robert Ellsberg, *All Saints* (New York: Crossroad, 1997), 371.

6. Maria Boulding, trans., *The Confessions* (Hyde Park, N.Y.: New City Press, 1997), 9.

7. Ibid., 131.

8. Howard Thurman, *Mysticism and the Experience of Love* (Wallingford, Penn.: Pendle Hill, 1961), 18.

9. Boulding, trans., 181.

10. Margaret Miles, *Desire and Delight* (New York: Crossroad, 1992), 77–78.

11. Boulding, trans., 26.

CHAPTER THREE

1. Walter Brueggemann, *Praying the Psalms* (Winona, Minn.: Saint Mary's Press, 1982), 15.

2. C. S. Lewis, *Reflections on the Psalms* (New York: Harcourt, Brace and World, Inc., 1958), 36.

3. Ibid., 3.

4. J. Clinton McCann Jr., *The New Interpreter's Bible,* 12 vols. (Nashville: Abingdon, 1996), 4:654; quoting Thomas G. Long, *Preaching and the Literary Forms of the Bible* (Philadelphia: Fortress, 1989), 47.

5. Lewis, *Reflections on the Psalms,* 41.

6. C. S. Lewis, *Surprised by Joy* (New York: Harcourt Brace Jovanovitch, 1955), 231.

7. Ibid.

8. Ibid.

9. Ibid.

10. A thorough account of the life and writings of Lewis can be found in the large, one-volume work by Walter Hooper, *C. S. Lewis Companion and Guide* (San Francisco: HarperSanFrancisco, 1996). Lewis's bedside marriage to Joy Davidman Gresham is reported on pages 79–83.

11. Colin Duriez, *The C. S. Lewis Handbook* (Eastbourne, Great Britain: Monarch, 1990), 64.

12. A. N. Wilson, *C. S. Lewis: A Biography* (New York: Fawcett Columbine, 1990), 269.

13. C. S. Lewis, *A Grief Observed* (New York: Bantam, 1961), 35.

14. C. S. Lewis, *The Problem of Pain* (New York: Macmillan, 1957), vii.

15. Ibid., viii.

16. Ibid., 81.

17. Hooper, 85–86.

18. Lewis, *A Grief Observed,* 25.

19. Ibid., 28.

20. Ibid., 34.

21. Ibid., 35.

22. Ibid., 2.
23. Ibid., 11.
24. Ibid., 16–17.
25. Ibid., 68.
26. Ibid., 71–72.

CHAPTER FOUR

1. J. Clinton McCann Jr., *The New Interpreter's Bible,* 12 vols. (Nashville: Abingdon, 1995), 4:235.
2. Bernard W. Anderson, *Understanding the Old Testament* (Englewood Cliffs, N.J.: Prentice-Hall, 1975), 506.
3. McCann, 4:1235.
4. Howard Thurman, *With Head and Heart* (New York: Harcourt Brace Jovanovitch, 1979), 20–21.
5. McCann, 4:1235.
6. Ibid.
7. Ron Eyre, *Ron Eyre on the Long Search* (New York: William Collins, 1979), 59–81. The quote is taken from the video on *The Long Search* entitled "Israel: The Chosen People."
8. McCann, 4:1238.
9. Ibid., 4:1237.
10. Thurman, *With Head and Heart,* jacket cover.
11. Howard Thurman, *The Creative Encounter* (New York: Harper and Row, 1954), 36.
12. Thurman, *With Head and Heart,* 24.
13. Howard Thurman, *Footprints of a Dream* (New York: Harper and Row, 1963), 96.
14. Thurman, *With Head and Heart,* 12.
15. Ibid., 20–21.
16. Benjamin E. Mays, "Tribute," *Debate and Understanding,* special edition, spring 1982, 87.
17. Thurman, *With Head and Heart,* 8–9.
18. Howard Thurman, *Disciplines of the Spirit* (New York: Harper and Row, 1963), 96.
19. Walter Fluker and Catherine Tumber, eds., *A Strange Freedom* (Boston: Beacon, 1998), 55.
20. Howard Thurman, *Deep River and the Negro Spiritual Speaks of Life and Death* (Richmond, Ind.: Friends United Press, 1975), 5.
21. Ibid., 70.
22. Ibid.
23. Ibid., 71.
24. Ibid., 72.
25. Ibid., 73.
26. Ibid., 76–77.
27. Ibid., 77.
28. Ibid.

CHAPTER FIVE

1. Terence Fretheim, *The New Interpreter's Bible,* 12 vols. (Nashville: Abingdon, 1994), 1:380.
2. Ibid., 1:389.
3. Ibid.
4. Ibid., 390.
5. Quoted by Shirley Du Boulay, *Tutu: Voice of the Voiceless* (Grand Rapids, Mich.: Eerdmans, 1988), 22–23.
6. Ibid., 45.
7. Ibid., 74.
8. Ibid., 56.
9. Desmond Tutu, *The Rainbow People of God* (Garden City, N.Y.: Doubleday, 1994), 187.
10. Ibid., 147.
11. Ibid.
12. Ibid., 148.
13. Ibid.
14. Ibid., 152.
15. Ibid., 154.
16. Ibid., 188.
17. Ibid., 268.

CHAPTER SIX

1. A. C. Purdy, *The Interpreter's Dictionary of the Bible,* 12 vols. (Nashville: Abingdon, 1962), 3:688.
2. Ibid.
3. Raymond E. Brown, *An Introduction to the New Testament* (Garden City, N.Y.: Doubleday, 1997), 447.
4. Ibid.
5. Ibid.
6. Julian of Norwich, *Showings—The Classics of Western Spirituality* (New York: Paulist, 1978), 149. I thank my student Katherine Pate for increasing my understanding of Julian.
7. Robert Ellsberg, *All Saints* (New York: Crossroad, 1997), 211.
8. Karen Armstrong, *Visions of God* (New York: Bantam, 1994), 176.
9. Ibid., 173.
10. Julian of Norwich, 21.
11. Armstrong, 179.
12. Ibid., 173.
13. Julian of Norwich, 149.
14. Ibid., 342.
15. Ibid.
16. Ibid., 340.
17. Sheila Upjohn, *Why Julian Now?* (Grand Rapids, Mich.: Eerdmans, 1997), 28.
18. Ibid., 29.
19. Ibid., 31.

CHAPTER SEVEN

1. Russell Pregeant, *Engaging the New Testament* (Minneapolis: Fortress, 1995), 236.
2. R. Alan Culpepper, *The New Interpreter's Bible*, 12 vols. (Nashville: Abingdon, 1995), 9:42.
3. Raymond E. Brown, *An Introduction to the New Testament* (Garden City, N.Y.: Doubleday, 1997), 229.
4. Ibid., 233.
5. Ibid.
6. Culpepper, 9:63.
7. Roland Bainton, *The Martin Luther Christmas Book* (Philadelphia: Muhlenberg, 1948), 13.
8. Hugh T. Kerr, ed., *Readings in Christian Thought* (Nashville: Abingdon, 1990), 138.
9. Bernhard Lohse, *Martin Luther: An Introduction to His Life and Thought* (Philadelphia: Fortress, 1986), 23.
10. Ibid.
11. I am indebted to my theological mentors Egon Gerdes, Paul Hessert, and Philip Watson for helping me to understand this most basic of all questions asked by Luther.
12. *Eerdmans' Handbook to the History of Christianity* (Grand Rapids, Mich.: Eerdmans, 1977), 360.
13. Lohse, 87.
14. Bradley P. Holt, *Brief History of Christian Spirituality* (Oxford: Lion, 1997), 91.
15. Kerr, 153.
16. Ibid.
17. Ibid.
18. Ibid., 154.
19. Ibid.
20. Ibid.
21. Ibid.
22. Ibid.

CHAPTER EIGHT

1. Bernhard W. Anderson, *Understanding the Old Testament* (Englewood Cliffs, N.J.: Prentice-Hall, 1975), 223.
2. Madeleine L'Engle, *Sold into Egypt* (Wheaton, Ill.: Harold Shaw, 1989), 11. I thank my student Machelle May, whose senior paper added to my appreciation for Madeleine L'Engle.
3. H. Stephen Shoemaker, *GodStories—New Narratives from Sacred Texts* (Valley Forge, Penn.: Judson, 1998), 65.
4. Anderson, 38–41.
5. Carole F. Chase, *Madeleine L'Engle, Suncatcher* (San Diego: LuraMedia, 1995), 19.
6. Ibid., 35.

7. Ibid., 44.
8. Ibid., 45.
9. Ibid., 72.
10. Ibid., 24.
11. Ibid., 25.
12. L'Engle, jacket cover.
13. Ibid., 235.
14. Terence Fretheim, *The New Interpreter's Bible,* 12 vols. (Nashville: Abingdon, 1994), 1:594.
15. L'Engle, 235.

CHAPTER NINE

1. Raymond E. Brown, *An Introduction to the New Testament* (Garden City, N.Y.: Doubleday, 1997), 126.
2. Pheme Perkins, *The New Interpreter's Bible,* 12 vols. (Nashville: Abingdon, 1995), 8:624.
3. Brown, 138.
4. Perkins, 8:621.
5. Marcus Borg, *Jesus: A New Vision* (San Francisco: Harper and Row, 1987), 130.
6. Dietrich Bonhoeffer, *No Rusty Swords* (New York: Harper and Row, 1965), 221.
7. Ibid., 78.
8. Eberhard Bethge, *Costly Grace* (New York: Harper and Row, 1979), 29.
9. Eberhard Bethge, "Turning Points in Bonhoeffer's Life and Thought" in Peter Vorkink, II, ed., *Bonhoeffer in a World Come of Age* (Philadelphia: Fortress, 1968), 80.
10. Ibid., 79.
11. Dietrich Bonhoeffer, *Letters and Papers from Prison,* enlarged ed. (New York: Macmillan, 1972), 4.
12. Eberhard Bethge, *Dietrich Bonhoeffer: A Biography* (New York: Harper and Row, 1954), 559.
13. Dietrich Bonhoeffer, *Life Together* (New York: Harper and Row, 1954), 13.
14. Eberhard Bethge, "The Last Days" in Dietrich Bonhoeffer, *Letters and Papers from Prison,* 3rd rev. ed. Quoted in Heinrich Ott, *Reality and Faith* (Philadelphia: Fortress, 1972), 257.
15. Bethge, *Dietrich Bonhoeffer,* 830.
16. See my discussion of Bonhoeffer's concept of Jesus as "the man for others" developed in his prison letters: William Apel, *Witnesses Before Dawn* (Valley Forge, Pa.: Judson, 1984), 15–29.
17. Bonhoeffer, *Letters and Papers from Prison,* 370.
18. Dietrich Bonhoeffer, *The Cost of Discipleship* (New York: Macmillan, 1960), 37.

CHAPTER TEN

1. Raymond E. Brown, *An Introduction to the New Testament* (Garden City, N.Y.: Doubleday, 1997), 383.
2. Ibid.

3. Ibid.
4. C. Clifton Black, *The New Interpreter's Bible,* 12 vols. (Nashville: Abingdon, 1998), 12:372.
5. Ibid., 374.
6. Ibid., 430.
7. *The Analytical Greek Lexicon* (Grand Rapids, Mich.: Zondervan, 1967), 401.
8. Albert C. Outler, *John Wesley* (New York: Oxford University Press, 1964), 6.
9. Albert C. Outler, *Theology in the Wesleyan Spirit* (Nashville: Tidings, 1975), 70.
10. Bradley P. Holt, *Brief History of Christian Spirituality* (Oxford: Lion, 1997), 111.
11. Ibid.
12. Hugh T. Kerr, ed., *Readings in Christian Thought* (Nashville: Abingdon, 1990), 193.
13. Ibid.
14. Outler, *Theology in the Wesleyan Spirit,* 83.
15. John Wesley, *A Plain Account of Christian Perfection* (London: Epworth, 1952), 38.
16. John Singleton, "Wesley Knew How to Beat Age," *The United Methodist—The Voice of United Methodists in the Oregon-Idaho Conference,* April 1999, 12.
17. Ibid.
18. Ibid.

CHAPTER ELEVEN

1. Donald E. Gowan, *The New Interpreter's Bible,* 12 vols. (Nashville: Abingdon, 1996), 7:412.
2. Bernhard W. Anderson, *Understanding the Old Testament* (Englewood Cliffs, N.J.: Prentice-Hall, 1975), 274.
3. Ibid., 277.
4. James M. Washington, ed., *A Testament of Hope—The Essential Writings of Martin Luther King Jr.* (San Francisco: Harper and Row, 1986), xvi.
5. This note from James Washington was written on the cover page of my copy of *A Testament of Hope.*
6. Washington, xviii.
7. Ibid., 421.
8. Robert Ellsberg, *All Saints* (New York: Crossroad, 1997), 153.
9. Washington, 421–22.
10. Ibid., xix.
11. Ibid.
12. Ellsberg, 152.
13. Ibid.
14. Washington, 290.
15. Hugh T. Kerr, ed., *Readings in Christian Thought* (Nashville: Abingdon, 1990), 389.
16. Martin Luther King Jr., *Strength to Love* (Philadelphia: Fortress, 1963), 4.

17. Ibid., 15.
18. Ibid., 134.
19. Ibid., 5.
20. Ibid., 113.
21. Ibid.

CHAPTER TWELVE

1. "Something beautiful for God" was a phrase used often by Mother Teresa and made famous by Malcolm Muggeridge's film and book about Mother Teresa which used the same phrase as a title.
2. M. Eugene Boring, *The New Interpreter's Bible,* 12 vols. (Nashville: Abingdon, 1995), 8:107–20.
3. Raymond E. Brown, *An Introduction to the New Testament* (Garden City, N.Y.: Doubleday, 1997), 172.
4. Boring, 8:457.
5. Ibid., 455.
6. Ibid.
7. Ibid., 424.
8. Ibid., 425.
9. *Hymns for the Family of God* (Nashville: Paragon Associates Inc., 1976), 677.
10. Anne Sebba, *Mother Teresa, Beyond the Images* (Garden City, N.Y.: Doubleday, 1997), 3–10.
11. Navin Chawla, *Mother Teresa, The Authorized Biography* (Boston: Element, 1992), 2.
12. Ibid., 3.
13. Mother Teresa, *Loving Jesus* (Ann Arbor, Mich.: Servant Publications, 1991), 141–42.
14. Robert Ellsberg, *All Saints* (New York: Crossroad., 1997), 393.
15. Ibid.
16. Ibid.
17. Mother Teresa, 119–20.
18. Chawla, 77.
19. Ibid., 155.
20. Ibid., 157.
21. Ibid., 73.
22. Ibid., 146.
23. Sebba, 242–68.
24. Chawla, 191.